914

10921

THE LISBON EARTHQUAKE

T. D. KENDRICK

THE LISBON EARTHQUAKE

J. B. LIPPINCOTT COMPANY
Philadelphia - - - - - - *New York*

Authorized American Edition

Printed in the United States of America

Library of Congress Catalog Card Number 57-6239

PREFACE

This book, written in the bicentenary year of the Lisbon earthquake, is not, as its rather ambitious title may suggest, a full history of the event. In fact, it is concerned mainly with the related themes of eighteenth-century earthquake-theology and the end of optimism. "Musings in the Carmo" such a book would probably have been called in 1855, the centenary year, a name that would have better indicated its limited content. The making of my own small collection of earthquake-pamphlets and sermons started me writing this work, but I could not have completed it if it had not been for the abundant help of friends most generously given. In Portugal these are Dr. José d'Almada, Dr. Carlos Mascarenhas de Azevedo, Mr. Martin Blake, the British Council's Representative in Lisbon, Eng. Castelo Branco of the Servicos Geológicos, R. Academia das Ciências, Dr. Carlos Estorninho, librarian of the British Council, and Dr. M. Santos Estevens, Director of the Biblioteca Nacional. Outside Portugal I have especially to thank Mr. Theodore Besterman, Director of the Institut Voltaire, Les Délices, Geneva, for valuable help with my Chapter Seven, which he was kind enough to read in typescript, and also Professor F. López Estrada of Seville University for help concerning my Spanish digression in Chapter Three. In this country I have many friends to thank among whom are Professor E. N. da C. Andrade, Professor C. R. Boxer, Sir Gavin de Beer, Mr. Marcus Cheke, Mr. L. C. G. Clarke, Mr. C. R. Dodwell, Mr. H. V. Livermore, Sir Alfred Munnings, Sir Lewis Namier, Señor Xavier de Salas, and several very kind colleagues in the British Museum. I have left to the last Mr. George West of the British Council whose detailed knowledge of eighteenth-century Lisbon is indispensable to anyone in this country writing on the subject. I cannot sufficiently thank Mr. West for the interest he has taken in this book and for the constant help he has given me.

T. D. KENDRICK

British Museum, W.C.1
  October 1955

CONTENTS

PLATES

TEXT FIGURES

Chapter One

LONDON, 1750

In October 1777 John Wesley said in a letter to his friend Christopher Hopper, "there is no divine visitation which is likely to have so general an influence upon sinners as an earthquake," and in this matter he spoke with experience and authority. In their correspondence at this time the two clergymen were no doubt referring to the earthquake that had recently alarmed Manchester and the neighbourhood on Sunday morning, 14 September; but Wesley, who was then seventy-four, was thinking also of the many past occasions on which he had seen a frightened people crowding into the churches after an earthquake in the last-minute hope of turning aside the wrath of God by urgent contrition and promises of future piety; for in his day the majority of the people believed that by the shuddering of the supposedly solid ground beneath their feet they were supernaturally commanded to listen in dread and shame to the holy voice of God.

Wesley, of course, had in his mind what we should call only light shocks; otherwise he would not have gone on to say in this same letter that an earthquake might be "no undesirable event." The Manchester earthquake exactly illustrated his point. It had done no real harm at all; but it had rumbled like thunder, shaken churches where folk were at morning service, so that some members of the congregation ran out of them in fear, and it had burst open doors and windows, brought a few chimneys down, and had made itself felt over a large area extending from Preston to Macclesfield. It caused great alarm, and was generally recognized as a dreadful announcement of divine vengeance likely to fall on the unhappy city. When nothing happened, and the short-lived fright was over, Dr. Beilby Porteous, the Bishop of Chester, published a letter to the people of Lancashire and Cheshire in which he exhorted them not to let the memory of their providential escape fade without proper reflection upon its significance. Divine admonitions were serious. "When the Almighty speaks in such tremendous language, he must not speak in vain." The Mancunians and their neighbours were too prosperous, and they had become sinful; but they had been spared the fate of Lisbon. God in His mercy had given them time to consider their position, and in a straightforward, manly way the Bishop called upon his people to give more thought to their spiritual lives. He suggested that there should be a revival of the neglected practice of family prayer.

All this was twenty-two years after the great Lisbon earthquake, but that terrible event was still remembered with awe, and was commonly mentioned, as the Bishop of Chester had done in his address, as something with which everybody was familiar. Possibly, the recollection of the murderous damage done in Lisbon on the morning of 1 November 1755 may have increased the fears caused by the light shock in Manchester in 1777; but it did not need a great earthquake to cause terror; in the eighteenth century a very mild earthquake indeed was frightening enough, even without a recent and close-at-hand example of the appalling results of a really serious earthquake. That this was so can be proved by the example of the two London earthquakes in February and March 1750, five years before Lisbon was destroyed. Very probably these were also in John Wesley's mind when he was writing to Hopper. He and Whitefield are said to have conducted all-night services on a shameful evening when London's earthquake-nerves had become almost uncontrollable.

The first occasion was a shock, or perhaps two shocks following each other in close succession, that was felt about noon on Thursday, 8 February. The Lord Chancellor, Hardwicke, sitting in Westminster Hall with the Courts of King's Bench and Chancery, and the counsellors with him, experienced a severe jolt. They thought for a moment that the great building was going to collapse on their heads. Newcastle House in Lincoln's Inn Fields so trembled that the Duke sent out to inquire what was happening. His servant went to the house of a neighbour, Dr. Gowin Knight, afterwards first principal librarian of the British Museum, and found him investigating the signs of disturbance in his own house; a grate that had been seen to move, a fire-shovel thrown down, a bed moved from its proper position, and so on. A lamp-lighter in Gray's Inn very nearly fell off his ladder. At Leicester House, where the Prince of Wales lived, it was believed that the foundations were sinking. Generally, throughout the City and in Westminster there was sudden consternation. People writing felt their desks lurch; chairs shook, doors slammed and windows rattled; pewter and crockery clattered on the shelves. A timber slaughter-house in Southwark collapsed, and chimneys fell in Leadenhall Street and elsewhere.

At first it was not believed that London was the victim of anything so awful as an earthquake, and there were theories, usual in such circumstances, about cannon-fire and powder-mills exploding. Then, when the truth was inescapable, it was said, reassuringly, that Sir Isaac Newton had known that this was going to happen, as he had calculated that Jupiter was going to approach so close to the earth in 1750 as possibly to brush it. "Jupiter, I think, has jogged us three degrees nearer the sun," said Horace Walpole, making a bad guess about this astronomical explanation, and it was found necessary to protest in the papers against the great philosopher's name being linked with such nonsense.

It was also thought by some people to be disgraceful that the London *Evening Post* for 10-13 February, as soon as most people had realized that the shock was caused by an earthquake, published only a bleak scientific note on the cause of such phenomena without making any reference to God, and the usual sequel of moralizing and pamphleteering began; but there was not time for much controversial talk to be published before London suffered another earthquake. Indeed, the whole event of Thursday, 8 February 1750, and its immediate aftermath, would have been of negligible importance were it not for the portentous fact that exactly four weeks later, on Thursday, 8 March, the blow fell a second time.

Even this was a feeble shock, though everyone agreed that it was much more violent than the first. It occurred in the early hours of the morning about 5:30 A.M., just as it was beginning to get light. Lord Chesterfield, who was in a deep sleep, was woken up with a bump. Horace Walpole thought there was somebody moving under his bed. People ran out into the streets, mostly in their night-clothes. Church bells were ringing of their own accord. Some chimneys had fallen. A pot-house in Gravel Lane, Lambeth, had lost part of its roof. Elsewhere two old houses had collapsed. A maid-servant in Charterhouse Square fell out of bed and broke her arm. There was an enormous smash in a china shop in St. James's Street, and a collection of valuable china belonging to a lady who lived in Piccadilly suffered heavily. In the high grounds of Grosvenor Square the shock was badly felt, and kitchen utensils were flung from shelves and dressers. Things were just as bad in outlying districts. The bailiff of Henry Fox, afterwards the first Lord Holland, telling his sheep about a quarter of a mile from Holland House actually saw the dry, solid ground move like a quagmire or quicksand, to the great alarm of the sheep and of the crows nesting near by.

This time the popular alarm was very much greater. It was all very well for scientifically minded persons to speculate about the physical cause of these recent blows, and to suggest that the last shock was not an earthquake at all, but an air-quake, as did the *General Advertiser* on 13 March, presumably basing their view on a letter by John Flamsteed, first Astronomer Royal, written in 1693 and now (in 1750) issued as a pamphlet; it was all very well to publish histories of earthquakes and classifications of them, proving that they are really frequent and familiar

natural events; it was all very well to show how lightly
London had escaped, to show that even in the most
ghastly disasters, for instance the earthquake in 1692 that
destroyed Port Royal, Jamaica, God does mercifully and
miraculously preserve many of His children. Londoners
were not disposed to calm themselves by such considerations. Something was going wrong with the country. There
had been the rebellion of 1745; there had been for some
years a terrible cattle-plague causing serious loss; there
had been "a sparing scourge" of locusts; and now, bang,
bang, came two earthquakes neatly spaced four weeks
apart. Londoners wanted to know what they ought to
think and what they ought to do. It was the Church that
gave them the required direction.

The most important of these pronouncements was the
letter addressed by the Bishop of London, Thomas Sherlock, to his clergy and people. It was published on 16
March. "Little philosophers," he said, "who see a little,
and but very little, into natural causes," might try to explain earthquakes without reference to God, but the
Bishop recognized the recent shocks as a divine warning that the time had come for Londoners to consider
their faults. The Gospel was rejected in spite of Protestant advantages; books were published that disputed or
ridiculed the great truths of religion, and such books were
not only welcomed in the wicked metropolis, but widely
circulated, even to our plantations in America. Blasphemous language was used openly in the streets. Lewd pictures illustrated all the abominations of the public stews,
and were tolerated. There was much homosexuality. People were crazy for amusement, and in one single news-

paper the Bishop had counted no less than fifteen advertisements for plays, dances, cock-fights, prize-fights, and so on, and this in Lent. Dr. Sherlock called for serious consideration of these shortcomings, but not for despair. God had not forgotten how to show mercy. We must now be genuinely sorry for our sins, and the Bishop showed how important it was that responsible people should set an example in good behaviour. Our rulers, magistrates, the clergy, heads of families, and parents generally, should recognize their duty, and a special attempt should be made to see that all young people received proper religious instruction.

The pamphlet was exactly right for the occasion. Some people, it is true, made a great deal of fun of it, and there was serious criticism to the effect that the Bishop should have remembered Christ's words about those killed by the fall of the tower in Siloam—*think ye that they were sinners above all men that dwelt in Jerusalem?* But generally the letter was accepted thankfully as the message of a brave and wise pastor. Men saw that the Bishop's rebuke was deserved, and they appreciated his concluding comfort and advice. A "very primitive discourse, and what is more, a very good one," said William Warburton, the future Bishop of Gloucester, at that time Preacher to Lincoln's Inn. In their pitiful state of earthquake-nerves and uneasy fear of an extremely severe impending disaster, ordinary folk found the Bishop of London's sharp medicine a steadying draught, and the pamphlet sold in enormous numbers, having several times to be reprinted. An anonymous supplement to it, by an author who thought the Bishop had not adequately covered the current vices, also went into a second edition.

Those who attended church had also been plainly directed in sermons, preached mostly on the Sunday after the second shock, 11 March. Thomas Secker, then Bishop of Oxford and afterwards Archbishop of Canterbury, preached in St. James's, Piccadilly, the church of which he was still Rector. He said that God had interwoven in His original grand creation various incidents that would alarm us and be lessons to us, and if one of these incidents came sharply upon us in the form of an earthquake, we must recognize it as specially applied to us, in this unhappy case London, the headquarters of wickedness and the shameful example thereof to the whole island. He had heard that people were considering leaving London to avoid what now seemed to be an imminent danger, and he asked if by such cowardice they hoped to fly from God. Fly from your iniquities, he said, if you would be safe. He urged his congregation to continue calmly with their daily occupations, remembering that the season was Lent, so that excessive pursuit of amusements must be avoided. What was needed most of all was a serious practical attention to their spiritual state.

The Reverend Dr. William Stukeley, M.D., F.R.S., preached on this same subject in his church, St. George's, Queen Square, Bloomsbury. He showed that earthquakes are singled out above all natural phenomena by their majesty and dreadful horror to mark an immediate operation of God's hand exercised in His divine anger. He was ready to discuss the physical causes of an earthquake with his fellow-scientists in the Royal Society; indeed, by 22 March he announced a theory that they were due to electricity, and three papers by him on this subject (the Society could not properly follow his meaning in the first one) are published in the *Philosophical Transactions* for 1750; but in his pulpit Stukeley had something much more important to say. Holy Scripture makes it quite clear that whatever their natural causes may be, earthquakes are God's instruments. This is why they always strike at populous cities, and not at uninhabited territories; and it is why they are specially frightful, inasmuch as they are sudden, unavoidable, and threaten us with a peculiarly dreadful form of death. God, therefore, was singularly merciful, considering the nature of London houses that sometimes collapse of their own accord, in merely giving London a good shake without toppling down one single inhabited house or killing one single person. The preservation of London was a miracle. God deliberately stopped the secondary causes that were producing the earthquake from producing the kind of earthquake that would have destroyed London.

What is God going to do next? asked William Agate, Lecturer of St. Lawrence Jewry, in a sermon preached in that church after the first shock. "Will he order winds to tear up our houses from their foundations and bury us in the ruins? Will he remove the raging distemper from the cattle and send the plague upon ourselves? Or (the Lord in his infinite mercy save us!) he may command the earth to open her mouth, and, the next time he ariseth to shake terribly the earth, command her to swallow us up alive, with our houses, our wives, our children, with all that appertains unto us."

The Reverend James Cox, D.D., until 1746 Master of Harrow School, a post from which he was dismissed as a result of his drunken and generally disgraceful behaviour, preached sermons in Hampstead and in Kensington that must have greatly frightened the congregations that sat under him. "We are now deservedly alarmed," he said, "and, for aught we know, may receive a peremptory summons that we *cannot play with* . . . to walk into eternity in the twinkling of an eye, whether sleeping or waking, who can tell?" What might be coming would prove a severe ordeal for the righteous, though they had the consolation of hope for better things in another world; but the unrighteous "are in a deplorable case indeed; they have nothing to feed upon but anguish and despair; they have nothing to raise their spirits; everything to deject them; their fears will carry them in sight of those chambers of darkness where the abuse of their reason and their evil deeds have led them, and must make them inexpressibly unhappy, because they will whisper the certainty that they will be for ever miserable." These thoughtless and abandoned people cannot ever expect to have the merits of Christ's precious blood applied for the pardon and expiation of their grievous transgressions. "Damnation will have its numbers, and come time enough, come when it will." His hearers may not have understood this baffling statement, but at least it sounded dreadful, and doubtless added to the terror of this solemn jeremiad.

Modern prophets had gone out of their way to multiply the reasons for dreading earthquakes. A remarkable book by Thomas Burnet (*c.* 1635-1715), Master of the Charterhouse, called *The Sacred Theory of the Earth,* first published in Latin in 1681, had reached its sixth edition by 1726, and was still read and discussed in the middle of the eighteenth century.[1] Burnet was of the opinion that this present earth, a very unsatisfactory second version of

[1] There was a seventh edition in 1759.

a first earth more or less destroyed by the Flood, was going to end in a great conflagration that would burn it right up, and when this happened, though the fire would naturally begin at Rome, the headquarters of Antichrist, England was going to be a particularly unpleasant spot because of its extensive coalfields that would burn so easily. The fact that from the smoke and ashes a vastly improved earth would be formed on the model of the first was not likely to be a consolation to the victims of the great fire, who could do nothing except look out anxiously for the signs that the awful day was approaching. Burnet said:

> The future combustion of the earth, according to the representations of scripture, is to be usher'd in and accompanied with all sorts of violent impressions upon Nature; and the chief instrument of these violences will be earthquakes. These will tear the body of the earth and shake its foundations; rend the rocks, and pull down the tall mountains; sometimes overturn, and sometimes swallow up towns and cities; disturb and disorder the elements, and make a general confusion in nature.

Burnet was dead, but living prophets of some scholastic importance and recognized position were likewise forecasting extreme woe to come that would be preceded by monitory earthquakes. One of these prophets was that most outspoken person, William Whiston (1667-1752), a divine and a scientist with a special bent for mathematics, who had for seven years been the successor of Sir Isaac Newton as Lucasian Professor of Mathematics at Cambridge, a position he lost owing to his unorthodox views on the Trinity. Whiston had evolved his own theory of the earth that he constantly developed in sermons, lectures, newspaper articles, and letters to the Press.

In Whiston's opinion the end of the world was fairly close at hand, but it was to be preceded by the restoration of the Jews to Jerusalem, and this event in turn was to be announced as imminent by ninety-nine tokens or signals, "vastly the greater part of which" had already been fulfilled. Prediction No. 92 was that there will happen a very terrible, but to good men a very joyful, great earthquake, when a tenth part of an eminent city will be destroyed. Seven thousand men of name and note are to perish.[2] The shock felt in February therefore presented this muddled-headed divine with an opportunity to expand his views (the great earthquake was to happen in London), and he gave a series of three lectures in London, the first of which on 6 March was on the ninety-nine signals, and the second, on their fulfilment, on 8 March, the day of the second shock. Lecture 3 on 10 March—on the horrid wickedness of the present age highly deserving such terrible judgement (a subject on which Mr. Whiston spoke with startling frankness and a great zest for naming culprits)—was of a kind calculated to leave his hearers with the impression that in spite of earnest exhortations to repentance and prayer, sinful London was too far plunged in iniquity for there to be any real hope of averting disaster.

The attendance in London at these three lectures were twenty-seven, sixty-five, and forty-three respectively; but a repetition at Tunbridge Wells was a failure, for on perceiving from Lecture No. 1 that the preacher was going

[2] Cf. Revelation xi. 13.

to discourage the place's major industries "gaming and other fooleries" nobody turned up to the following discourses. In London, too, Whiston was no doubt rather a comic figure. "The greatest mischief the earthquakes have hitherto done is only widening the crack in old Will Whiston's noddle," remarked Warburton in a letter; but there was at the time a great interest in Biblical prophecy, and though some people might laugh, Whiston's views were talked about; after all, they came from a man of immense learning who had an established reputation as a theologian, Biblical historian, editor of *Josephus,* and an astronomer, mathematician, and physicist. He *might* be right, and his vehement utterances contributed sensibly to the prevalent malaise.

Most of the general earthquake-literature published at the time was of the kind to spread further despondency. Painful accounts appeared of the 1692 earthquake that had destroyed Port Royal, Jamaica, described in one pamphlet as "the most terrible earthquake that has ever happened since the creation of the World," and in the middle of February a new edition was published of the *True and Particular Relation of the Dreadful Earthquake —— at Lima —— and Callao,* a translation from the Spanish in a handsome 5*s.* book that described a catastrophe in Peru that happened in 1746, only four years previously, which was "one of the most dreadful, perhaps, that ever befel this earth since the general Deluge." It had caused great destruction in Lima and had virtually obliterated the port, Callao, by gigantic seismic inundation. There five thousand people perished and only two hundred were saved. "Not the least sign of its former figure does now appear: on the contrary, vast heaps of sand and gravel occupying the spot of its former situation, it is at present become a spacious strand."

This disquieting book was followed early in March by a second edition of the *Practical Reflections on the late Earthquakes* by John Shower, the Nonconformist divine, originally published in 1693, a decent, careful, but excessively gloomy little book costing 1s. 6d. It ends with a forcible expression of the view that whatever God in His mercy may do in the way of sparing the nation, for all unrepentant sinners nevertheless "it is most certain that security is a presage of ruin." Such people cannot be long out of the grave or out of Hell, and are in danger of damnation every hour, terrible remediless torment under the everlasting curse of God.

It is sad to hear of this, sad to foresee it, to consider it, to think of it; but it will be much sadder to suffer, and to feel it. And be not deceived, it is not the less certain, because it is yet future. You are now alive, and do not see the grave digged for you, and yet you must die. And as certainly do I know from the word of God, who cannot lie, that *except you repent, you must perish,* and that forever.

There was little in the numerous cheaper pamphlets, written for the occasion, that could have made any sort of contribution to the nervous reader's peace of mind. Nor were the *Verses on the late Earthquakes: address'd to Great Britain* in any sense consoling. The poet was "strongly apprehensive of something yet more disastrous at hand." It was understandable that other wicked lands should suffer earthquakes.

> *Jamaica shou'd* be shook! a Land
> Like *Sodom, all* impure!

> That Earthquakes rock *Italic* Ground,
> Scarce strikes us with Amaze!

And so on. But now Britain, because of its wickedness, is running a similar risk.

> Own it! (but with a *blush*) "No Realm
> Like *ours!* so *vile!* so *vain!*
> See! to the *Dunghill* from the *Helm*
> Extends the *moral* stain!"

Benjamin Stillingfleet also gave the Londoners a poem, *Some Thoughts occasioned by the late Earthquakes,* for the benefit of those who, while they might be inclined to read verse, were not likely to wade through the prose of the Bishop of London's letter with proper attention. He too said the sinful people were in the greatest possible danger. Britain had thought herself immune from disasters such as affect other nations, but now she knows from recent convincing and alarming events that God:

> Wanteth not stones to execute His wrath
> Wherever Vengeance calls: the gaping Gulph
> Shall overwhelm us if He give the word.

Understandably, after all this there were a good many people in London who were really nervous and apprehensive. And this time, instead of their fears quickly disappearing, as usually happens after a light shock, they lingered and increased. The tidiness of an interval of exactly four weeks between the two shocks was now considered to be unpleasantly mysterious. It is in fact this coincidence that in the end gave these two very mild earthquakes an unexpectedly discreditable importance in London history, for in consequence of their remarkable timing a lunatic lifeguardsman called Mitchell went about the town circulating a prophecy that at a further interval of four weeks, that is on the night of Wednesday, 4 April, or on the morning of Thursday, 5 April, London was going to be destroyed by a third, and this time completely devastating, earthquake. This at once eclipsed the vaguer lucubrations of all the other prophets of woe. London's time was up, and the date of its obliteration settled. In their long history Londoners have not shown themselves to be a characteristically nervy and timorous people, but on this occasion earthquake-fright caused an ignoble panic. As the supposedly fateful day approached, the general alarm grew greater and more hysterical; there was much talk of leaving the capital, and some people did indeed begin to pack up and go.

The clergy spoke out bravely against this cowardice, led by Thomas Secker in his sermon on 11 March in St. James's, Piccadilly; but the most urgent rebuke, preached on Sunday, 1 April, when the panic was approaching its height, was the inspiring sermon of Roger Pickering, F.R.S., pastor of a church of Dissenters in Silver Street and Lord's Day Evening Lecturer at Salter's Hall, a sermon that he succeeded in getting into print before 5 April, the day of the expected shock. His theme was the omnipresence of God. "If I take the wings of the morning, and dwell in the uttermost parts of the sea: even there shall thy hand lead me, and thy right hand shall hold me." The psalmist, said the preacher, knew that no distance could separate him, no velocity remove him, from divine

vengeance if guilty, nor put him beyond the protection
of God, were he a righteous man.

Pickering was a scientist, and he asked what maximum
flight the lovely words quoted could be fancifully assumed to mean. Perhaps a speed that was that of the velocity of light, and a distance of a full half-circle of the
globe; 10,800 miles at something like 10,000,000 miles a
minute. The longest possible flight on earth in the short-
est possible time, say one-thousandth of a minute. But it
would be no use; so what good could be this pitiful emi-
gration to places a few miles from London? The preacher
then recited to his people the great hymn to creation contained in the 104th psalm; he showed that God was universally present throughout His creation, today as at the
beginning, and presided over its destiny in all particulars,
and that all men were under the constant government and
influence of God. Christians must not be afraid. We must
trust God. In the magnificent end to his sermon, Pickering said:

> I *adjure* you, by the *Interest* of that *Gospel* you pro-
> fess, by the *Credit* of that *Faith* on which you rest your
> Souls, that, with *humble Hearts,* but with *Christian
> Confidence,* in your respective Stations ON THE SPOT
> where *Providence* has placed you, YE WAIT the WILL
> OF GOD.

It was, however, too late for this noble command to
steady the nerves of a thoroughly frightened people. The
exhortations of so many clergy, the example of men of
high position, and the derision of the wits, did not succeed in preventing the shameful exodus. After all, the
people had been told plainly enough that the warning

of the shocks was specially directed to the inhabitants of the cities of London and Westminster; they were the guilty culprits; they were told too (Dr. Stukeley had made a special point of this) that earthquakes strike only at densely populated places; and they were told that they bury indiscriminately both the righteous and the unrighteous. Under these circumstances who was going to be foolish enough to stay in a doomed town? The obvious thing to do was to get out of London as soon as possible. So nervousness increased, and finally there was a truly shameful panic. On the eve of the prophesied disaster Horace Walpole said, "This frantic fear prevails so much that within these three days 730 coaches have been counted passing Hyde Park Corner with whole parties removing into the country." The roads were crowded with refugees. Lodging was unobtainable in safe places like Windsor and other outlying towns and villages. Some who did not go right out of town camped in near-by fields or sat in coaches or in boats for the night. Women made "earthquake gowns" for a vigil in the open. A contemporary cartoon (Pl. I) is a fair comment on what must have been a deplorable scene, though it is spoilt for us by the fact that the refugees passing the top of St. James's Street are going eastwards instead of, as is more likely, westwards. We hear that a third of the inhabitants of London fled, no doubt a great exaggeration; [3] but people certainly escaped from the town in very large numbers. And when nothing happened on 5 April, many

[3] This is Stukeley's estimate. "Publicus" in the *General Evening Post*, 17-19 April, said that "perhaps 100,000 persons" left their houses to take refuge in Hyde Park on the night of Wednesday, 4 April.

stayed away until after Sunday the eighth, in case the sequence was to be 8 February, 8 March, and 8 April.

One of the refugees explained her conduct. This was Lady Bradshaigh, who escaped to Reading and wrote from there to Samuel Richardson, who, she hoped, had at least left his town house in Salisbury Court, Fleet Street, together with Mrs. Richardson, for his house at North End, Hammersmith.

> I could not help reflecting [she wrote on 25 March], how many valuable people I left in a situation threatened with a calamity I was flying from; which gave me infinite pain. The Bishop of Oxford, I hear, in his sermon . . . called it a *presumption* in any one who left London on this occasion. A presumption it would be in those who remove with an assurance of safety; but, if a person's mind will be more at ease in one place than another, it may argue a weakness, but I know no harm in chusing that place. I religiously believe God's providence is over all His works; and on that every serious person must depend, whatever situation he may be in. He has also given us means to provide for our safety, and permits us to fly from danger, though, from our erroneous judgement, we may run into a greater. God hath warned us to flee from the wrath to come, and if we take that for a warning, which, in reality, is not one, surely in that we sin not.

Lady Bradshaigh did not wish to compare London with Sodom, for London no doubt contained many good people; but because of its size it also contained a proportionately large number of bad people, so it was just as well to keep away, and, setting aside all other considerations, London, by reason of its crowded and insecure buildings, "is, of all other places, to human appearance, the most dangerous." The Richardsons refused to budge. Lady Bradshaigh pointed out that there was never any long space of time between shocks, and it was obviously prudent to keep at a distance from the place of alarm. She was glad, however, to be able to say that the presumptuous prophecy of the lifeguardsman had not influenced her at all.

After they had at last considered it safe to return, the refugees found they had come back to face a very bad Press. The *Remembrance* called their behaviour irrational and impious, and was much concerned for the national dignity. The *Daily Advertiser* observed in verse that "low stupid panics speak a pigmy race"; the *London Magazine* observed that such imaginary fears should not have taken the place of the proper reflections due on such an occasion, and the *Gentleman's Magazine* said "so far, even to their wit's end, had their superstitious fears, or their guilty conscience driven them." The London *Evening Post,* under reproof for tardiness in recognizing God's personal intervention on the occasion of the first earthquake, now spoke out bravely about these cowards. "Let such weak minds consider that when God resolves to punish a sinful nation, He alone knows the proper time of doing it . . . a time that no human sagacity could ever foresee or foretell."

The lifeguardsman was sent to the madhouse. The public fright was quickly forgotten, and folk resumed unconcernedly their ordinary lives. In the preface to the pamphlet edition [4] of his *Philosophy of Earthquakes, Natural and Religious,* a paper read to the Royal Society in December 1750, Stukely said he was continuing his investigation in order that the two recent shocks should not be so quickly forgotten, as they seemed to have been, by "the giddy multitude." But thoughtful people did not easily forget the controversy between those who believed God had purposely given London two sharp jolts in order to remind the city of its iniquity and those who did not think God had shown any immediate interest in London in this remarkable way. This dispute did not develop unexpectedly in magnitude or bitterness in 1750, nor did it even remotely approach the painful urgency that the problem presented after the Lisbon earthquake in 1755. But it was there, and it rankled, disturbing orthodox clerical minds that had become singularly sensitive to any doctrine that seemed to belittle revealed religion and to be in agreement with deistic thought.

Some of the clergy merely asserted the immediate divine origin of earthquakes without theological or philosophical comment. That it is God who shakes the earth "is as great and evident a truth as that he doth exist," said the Dissenter Thomas Newman, preaching at Crosby Square, and he dismissed all the talk about subterranean caverns, inflammable vapours, and so forth, as irrelevant prattle. Theophilus Lobb, Nonconformist theologian, declared in his *Sacred Declarations* (1750) that "earthquakes are the productions of the almighty power of God, and happen only when and where He commands

---

[4] Stukeley's sermon at St. George's and his two Royal Society papers were published together as a pamphlet in 1750; they were re-issued after the Lisbon earthquake with an additional paper read to the Royal Society on 15 January 1756.

them to happen." In other words, as Dr. John Allen put it, since nature is God-created and God-governed, "the philosophy of nature is but knowledge of the *art* of God."

But many of the clergy had much more to say on this particular subject than a simple declaration of opinion, knowing that if they assured their hearers that God had a part as an immediate agent in these or any other earthquakes, an enlightened and inquisitive mid-eighteenth-century society would expect from the preacher a reasonable theodicy, a justification of the God who was alleged to govern His people by the sharp threat of an impending earthquake and, indeed, by the appalling savagery of a great earthquake itself.

The clergy were quarrelling with *philosophers* and not with scientists; indeed, clergy and scientists could not even be marshalled in opposite camps. Whiston was a scientist and had held Newton's chair; Theophilus Lobb was a physician and F.R.S.; Pickering was F.R.S.; and Chandler became one in 1754. Stukeley, also F.R.S., lectured to the Royal Society, and his friend Stephen Hales, the Curate of Teddington, was another famous scientist divine, F.R.S., and D.D., who addressed the Society on the subject of earthquakes, saying he could pass without delay to a scientific discussion of their cause, as the other side of the matter had been adequately treated in the Bishop of London's letter. Indeed, it is the case that many clergy agreed that some earthquakes were best explained by their natural scientific causes and not as an act that was supernaturally controlled, for God had created this world in such a way that its perfect ordering, arrangement, and development made earthquakes necessary as part of His original plan for its physical behaviour. The

Archbishop of Dublin, William King (1650-1729), had written in his *Essay on the Origin of Evil:* [5]

> Neither are *Earthquakes, Storms, Thunder, Deluges* and *Inundations*—Arguments against the Wisdom and Goodness of God. They are sometimes sent by a just and gracious God for the punishment of Mankind; but often depend on other natural Causes, which are necessary, and could not be removed without greater Damage to the whole. These Concussions of the Elements are indeed prejudicial, but more Prejudice could arise to the Universal System by the Absence of them.

The scientists had in their own right a considerable public in the learned world accustomed to their views. The entry made under the heading "earthquake" in Ephraim Chambers's *Cyclopædia* (second edition, 1738) begins, "in natural history a vehement shake—of the earth; from natural causes," and there is no suggestion that these "greatest and most formidable phenomena of nature" could possibly have any other cause; and the account of earthquakes in the first volume of Buffon's already popular *Histoire Naturelle* (1749) was a part of his systematic explanation of nature solely in terms of natural cause and effect. The clergy, therefore, had a good opportunity for accepting a changing view about the significance of earthquakes and attempting to calm their agitated congregations by an assurance that the two earthquake-shocks might after all have been natural phenomena. But there were strong reasons for not doing so. They did think the sins of the age merited divine rebuke; they found the majority of the people tearfully ready to ac-

[5] Third edition (Cambridge, 1739), p. 188, trans. by Edmund Law. King's *De Origine Mali* was first published in 1702.

cept the earthquakes as such a rebuke; and, above all, the common interpretation of them in this sense enormously strengthened the apparent case of the Church against the deism of the "little philosophers."

This was still an important consideration. In the middle of the eighteenth century it was not the forgetfulness of unheeding people, not the sturdy unbelief of the atheist, nor the ribaldry of flippant folk that constituted separately or together the worst danger the clergy had to oppose. They knew well enough how to deal with such ordinary enemies of the faith. It was against the followers of natural religion that the earthquake-panic offered a crushing argument, if it were agreed that God was by means of these earthquakes directly speaking to His sinful children on earth; for in natural religion an aloof and unapproachable God stands coldly away from His creation, letting it work itself according to originally established natural laws, and this kind of God had to be challenged and denounced by the ministers of a revealed religion based on the central doctrines of the Incarnation and Atonement, and the use of sacramental worship. Natural religion could not be anything else than a subtle and very serious menace to orthodox Christianity, and the hostility shown to Matthew Tindal's outspoken book, *Christianity as Old as the Creation*, published in 1730, is a proof that the danger of deism had not by this time passed harmlessly away.

Therefore, in addition to the pastoral care expected from them, the clergy had to assert convincingly that God loved His people and presided over their destinies to the extent of warning them by sharp punishment when they had been, as now, excessively wicked. The necessity for punishment was not difficult to explain with so many sinners already on their knees. But a severe earthquake as a just punishment of mankind is not so easily explained. In fact, before asking why such an indiscriminately cruel event is used by God for the purpose of His moral government of the world, comes an understandable question about the competence of a Creator who made a world so imperfect that such horrible proofs of its faulty structure were thus revealed. Nevertheless current optimistic thought of the period had a ready answer to both questions, one that was no longer to be found only in the lofty thought of Leibniz, Bolingbroke, and Pope, and other of the more illustrious philosophers, but was ordinary preacher's material. In the first place, an earthquake may seem to be a disastrous event overthrowing the essential basic security of a settled order of nature, and may therefore appear to be a proof of the imperfection of God's work at the creation of the world; but this is because we cannot even dimly comprehend the colossal plan involved in the act of creation. This thought was stated many times at many different levels of society in various ways. As an example, John Clarke, afterwards Dean of Salisbury, said in his Boyle Lectures in 1719: [6]

In the ordinary Works of human Art and Contrivance, we see how difficult it is to account for any particular Part in most of them, without knowing the whole Composition: As in a Clock or a Watch; He who should go about to condemn the Shape or Use of any particular Wheel, the Situation or Design of which was not

[6] Clarke's sermons were called *An Enquiry into the Cause and Origin of Evil*, Letsome and Nicholl. *Boyle Lectures*, III, pp. 168-69. London, 1739.

at all understood by Him; it would but discover his own Ignorance and not at all reflect upon the Workman. We need not therefore be surprised, if in our Survey of the Universe, we be often at a loss to account for many Things that we observe there.

And, further:

We judge of the Knowledge and Skill of the Workman by his Performances; or by what we experience of his Skill, we judge what is likely to be the Effect of it: and *these* mutually assist each other. So likewise in the System of the World, or the whole Frame of Nature; we know that a Being infinitely wise, all-powerful and good, cannot be the Author of any Thing, but what is worthy of those Perfections to create: And consequently, since every Thing that *is*, was made by Him, it must originally and as He made it, be *very good;* that is, fit for that End and Purpose for which it was designed.

An earthquake may not therefore be, as an imperfection in the natural order, an evil thing; and, arguing on the same lines, it may not be morally, if used as a punishment, an unjust thing. In 1736 in one of the greatest English theological works of the first half of the eighteenth century, *The Analogy of Religion, Natural and Revealed, to the Constitution and Course of Nature,* Joseph Butler, who in this year, 1750, two years before his death, had just become Bishop of Durham, wrote:

Suppose then, that there are things in the system of the world, and plan of Providence relating to it, which taken alone would be unjust: yet it has been shown unanswerably, that if we could take in the reference, which these things may have to other things present, past, and to come; to the whole scheme, which the things objected against are part of; these very things might, for aught we know, be found to be, not only consistent with justice, but instances of it.

Indeed, it has been shown—not only possible that this may be the case, but credible that it is.[7]

The two earthquakes of 1750 were accordingly regarded by Bishop Secker in his aforementioned sermon as examples of incidents intended to alarm us from time to time that for our benefit had been *woven* by God into His original scheme of creation. Another preacher, the Nonconformist Samuel Chandler preaching in Old Jewry on 11 March, said that earthquakes and like disasters are operations of the laws of nature determined by God, their "proper agent," at the time of the first origin of nature, and are constantly maintained in their activity and vigour by Him in order that they may exert themselves and produce their effect at those predetermined periods in which God foresaw they would best promote the purposes of His moral providence and government. In effect, then, what people were told was that, having due regard to the infinite wisdom of God, earthquakes, however terrible, must be accepted as something beneficial in two ways: physically beneficial to the earth as a purge or as an enrichment of local mineral resources; and beneficial morally, on a long view, to the human race that had to endure the temporary suffering they caused.

All is for the best in the best of all possible worlds. Even an earthquake. And this was the Leibnizian view, preached by Chandler and others in London in 1750, that

[7] Part II, Ch. VIII, p. 306, ed. Halifax, new edition 1844.

had to be examined just over five years later in desperate moods of anxiety, pity, and terror, when an earthquake happened that by its savage destruction of a famous city and its unheeding massacre of the inhabitants most profoundly shocked not only London but all the world.

In this turmoil of rumours, prophecies, panicky fears, sermonizing, and pamphleteering, there were, as is to be expected, many who preferred to stand aside from the commotion and watch the spectacle of their fellow-citizens making fools of themselves. There was much flippancy. Some ladies of Westminster were alleged to be "so deliberately, so ludicrously profane in these awful judgements" as to send each other invitations to earthquake-parties.[8] The members of White's were described by a parson as such an impious set of people that, if the Last Trump were to sound "they would bet puppet-show against Judgement." Moreover, as they deserved, the refugees were mocked mercilessly, and the clergy blamed for taking an unfair advantage of the people's alarm.

I think the parsons have lately used the Physicians very ill [wrote David Hume to John Clephane, a Scottish medical man], for in all the common terrors of mankind you used both to come in for a share of the profit: but in their new fear of earthquakes, they have left you out entirely, and have pretended alone to give prescriptions to the multitude.—I see . . . a pastoral letter of the Bishop of London, where, indeed, he recommends certain pills, such as fasting, prayer, repentance, mortification, and other drugs, which are entirely to come from his own shop.

[8] *Old England*, Saturday, 7 April 1750. An anonymous letter signed Eubalus (? written by Whiston).

Horace Walpole said in a letter that the clergy "who have had no windfalls of a long season," have "driven horse and foot" into the opinion that the two earthquakes were a divine judgement.

There has been a shower of sermons and exhortations. Secker, the Jesuitical Bishop of Oxford began the mode. He heard the women were all going out of town to avoid the next shock; and so, for fear of losing his Easter offerings, he set himself to advise them to await God's pleasure in fear and trembling. But what is more astonishing, Sherlock, who has much better sense, and much less of the Popish confessor, has been running a race with him for the old ladies and has written a pastoral letter of which 10,000 were sold in two days; and 50,000 have been subscribed for since the first two editions. You never read so impudent, so absurd a piece! This earthquake, which has done no hurt, in a country where no earthquake ever did any, is sent, according to the Bishop, to punish bawdy prints, bawdy books . . . gaming, drinking—(no, I think, drinking and avarice, those orthodox vices are omitted), and all other sins, natural or not. . . ."[9]

The Devil (in an anonymous pamphlet) wrote a letter of congratulation and advice to the inhabitants of Great Britain, particularly those of the two cities of London and Westminster, in the matter of their conduct before and after the late earthquakes. Before then he had been delighted with the British: "we know not which is most worthy of our admiration, whether your unparalleled refinements in all kind of luxury and debauchery,

[9] *Letters of Horace Walpole,* ed. Toynbee, II, p. 435.

or your sagacity in reasoning away every principle of virtue and honour. . . . France and Rome compared to you are but petty candidates for Hell"; but after the first quake the Devil feared the British would take fright and truly repent their evil ways, and he was accordingly overjoyed to discover that they were only momentarily scared. The second shock was a new risk from his point of view. "Fear drove you to your temples, and the few enemies we have among your priests improved the occasion and thundered repentance from the pulpits, and fear or shame even influenced the rest to the like practice"; but, once more, Hell was reassured. As soon as the day of the predicted third shock was safely past, the people recovered their equanimity, and Hell smiled at their renewed wickedness. "Return then, my dear children, to your wonted course . . . laugh at them who would be serious with you. Confound them with second causes—"

A "Gentleman in Town," Walpole's friend Richard Bentley, in another pamphlet published anonymously, described in the form of a letter to a country friend a pretended third earthquake. When it happened the first man sunk was the Bishop of London, though he might have escaped if he had not been so busy distributing copies of his letters. The Duke of Newcastle was next, the place of his disappearance being marked by scatterings of papers and red tape. Then followed a long list of other notable casualties, and the news that Mr. Whiston had set out on foot for Dover on the way to Jerusalem to meet the millennium.

The joke proved so popular that a second letter was published. White's was swallowed up, Mr. Tuff wagering that all the members were going to Hell; the Inns of

Court were all sunk, and it was ordered that no lawyers
were to be rescued, though they had since begun to
swarm as usual. The Speaker was dug up with the mace
in his hands. A wide breach opened between St. James's
Palace and Leicester House (the residence of the Prince
of Wales, who had quarrelled with the King). Brown
Willis was dug up by order of the Antiquarians. Mr.
Gideon in the City (Sampson Gideon, the financier)
threatens still another quake if his brethren do not sub-
scribe their four per cents quick enough. The Commis-
sioners of Westminster Bridge have ordered the earthquake to be entered in their books as a glorious excuse
for the next sinking pier (the sinking of a pier had been
prominent news in 1748). The Middlesex justices, having
been asleep for many years, have woken up and condemned a masquerade at Ranelagh, advising young people not to attend it; but in order not to offend the pro-
prietors, they kept their advice secret till the day before
it took place, so that the tickets might all be sold before
the young people knew it would be improper to use them.
This was the Venetian Masquerade announced for 17
April, Tuesday after Easter, and the intention of hold-
ing it seemed to some very indignant people to mark that
wholehearted return to London's evil practices on which
the Devil had commented with so much satisfaction. It
was postponed till 24 April, and then to the twenty-fifth,
and as a result of the Middlesex magistrates' action took
place without gaming tables and "other instruments of
fraud."

It is said that the first half of the eighteenth century,
with its enlightenment, its optimism, its cult of happiness,

and its content with the *status quo,* was a fortunate age, so much so that it might be preferred to all other times in the past as the one in which a sensible man might elect to live. Referring to the positive stimulus of a new manner of thinking, Professor Willey has said that in the early and middle years of the century "the wealthy and educated of Europe must have enjoyed almost the nearest approach to earthly felicity ever known to man," [10] and in England the reign of the first two Georges has been described by Professor Williams as an "oasis of tranquillity," "an age of stability in politics, in religion, in literature, and in social observances." [11] In that comfortable world it may have been the case that an earthquake was, except for the Day of Judgement, the most terrible thing that could happen to man, and from the story of the two London earthquakes of 1750 we see plainly what great alarm could be caused even by light shocks and no more than the fear of a greater earthquake to come. For, truly, an earthquake *is* a terrifying thing, even without a death-roll and destruction. Almost all the ordinary actions of our lives demand as an essential prerequisite that the ground should remain firm and motionless under our feet and beneath the foundations of our houses. The total overthrow of mental security that results from any perceptible indication that it will not do so is itself in the highest degree alarming; and if to this be added the unpredictable suddenness of the event, the instant consideration that one is powerless in its presence, and the

[10] Basil Willey: *The Eighteenth Century Background,* p. 44. London, 1953. On this subject see also p. 182 *infra.*
[11] Basil Williams: *The Whig Supremacy,* p. 1. Oxford, 1939.

dreaded possibility of its recurrence, we can understand why there should be fright at even a mild tremor.

From the first century to the present day men have felt much the same about an earthquake,[12] but for the ordinary people of the middle eighteenth century the special horror of the event was still the awful belief that an earthquake was a deliberate sign to them from a wrathful God. No attempt at a scientific explanation had as yet made an earthquake in the general consciousness an understandable happening, like a flood or a fire. Even an eclipse was still supernaturally awe-inspiring to many people. Stukeley said in his sermon at St. George's, Queen Square:

> We saw not long ago, what an effect was produced by a solar eclipse, tho' it was expected long before. We had the prediction, and calculation about it in all our almanacs; yet there was an universal seriousness that followed it. All that morning, we could walk the streets, without hearing an oath, and the churches were full, in time of prayer.[13]

An earthquake remained therefore for the majority of people an event "instinct with deity," terrible because of the holiness of God. If it aroused pity, sympathy, and charity towards those who suffered in such a disaster, it aroused also a violently emotional theological reckoning, expressed in hysterical repentance and agitated speculation about man's relation to God and about God's purpose for this world. The sinner stood sharply rebuked, and

[12] Cf. Seneca: *Natur. Quaest,* vi, 1.
[13] William Stukeley: *Philosophy of Earthquakes,* p. 40. London, 1750.

terrified; the churches filled, and the parson had to chide and comfort his congregation. That was the result of two light shocks of 1750. And the religious apprehensions of the people and the concern of the clergy were also dominant emotions when in the second half of November 1755 the terrible news arrived in London that on the first day of the month the city of Lisbon had been destroyed by a great earthquake with enormous loss of life.

Chapter Two

THE LISBON
EARTHQUAKE

The Lisbon earthquake lasted about ten minutes. It began about 9:30 A.M. on All Saints' Day, Saturday, 1 November 1755, and gave the town three distinct shocks separated by intervals of about a minute. The first alarm was a rumbling noise that many people said sounded like that of exceptionally heavy traffic in an adjacent street, and this was sufficient to cause great alarm and make the buildings tremble; then there was a brief pause, and a devastating shock followed, lasting over two minutes, that brought down roofs, walls, and façades of churches, palaces, and houses and shops in a dreadful deafening roar of destruction. Close on this came a third trembling to complete the disaster, and then a dark cloud of suffocating dust settled fog-like on the ruins of the city. It had been a clear, bright morning, but in a few moments the day turned into the frightening darkness of night, and when the dust began to settle ten or fifteen minutes later and people began to crawl about in the wreckage, it was seen that fires had broken out in several parts of the shattered town and threatened the city with a huge consuming conflagration; and then as these fires grew there occurred a dreadful event on the water-front about an hour after the first triple shock; for the waters of the Tagus rocked and rose menacingly, and then poured in three great towering waves over its banks, breaking with their mightiest impact on the shore between the Alcântara docks and the Terreiro do Paço.

To make worse this cruel day in which so many unfortunate people were crushed to death, burnt to death, or drowned, the earthquake was followed by several after-shocks, which were generally taken to be warnings that an even more awful disaster might at any minute complete the destruction of the town. In fact, they were not, it seems, very serious quakes, but one of them that happened about 11 A.M., just before the breaking of the seismic waves over the Lisbon quays and foreshore, did heavy damage in the western town, shattering the Church of Santa Catarina on the hill close to the river and bringing down the east end of the Church of São Paulo, where a large number of refugees lost their lives. There was also a frightening after-shock about noon, felt sharply in northern Lisbon; but the principal ruin of the famous city was the work of the triple quake before 10 A.M.

The Lisbon earthquake, if measured by the destruction caused and its death-roll, was not one of the greatest disasters of its kind that have ever happened. India, China, and Japan have experienced earthquakes much more terrible, for example the dreadful Kwanto earthquake of 1923 that came near to destroying the whole of Tokyo and Yokohama and killed one hundred thousand people; but the earthquake of 1 November 1755 was nevertheless a colossal seismic disturbance that was felt over so large an area that it caused general alarm and astonishment and a great output of scientific speculation. It shook, for the most part severely, the whole south-west corner of Portugal, doing great damage to Setúbal and Sácavem, and in the southern coast of the Algarve the towns of Lagos, Faro, and Tavira (Fig. 1). There was also a tremendous earthquake in North Africa in the area of Fez and Mequinez, where the destruction was catastrophic and there was a heavy loss of life; less severely it was felt as far away as Algiers on the African coast, and all over south-west Spain and Portugal from Coimbra to Seville and Cádiz; outside that area it was felt at many other places in central and southern Spain from Madrid to Granada, Guadix, Málaga, and Gibraltar. It caused noticeable shocks in northern Spain, and in France certainly as far as Bordeaux, and probably farther north (Fig. 2). Evidence of the full extent of the earthquake is unsatisfactory; but shocks were reported at places like Lyons and Strasbourg and in Switzerland and North Italy, and also in Normandy and Brittany and the Scilly Islands. It was said, probably erroneously, to have been felt in Derbyshire and in Scotland. The sea-waves caused by the earthquake certainly reached England and Ireland, where they were recorded about 2 P.M., and they reached the West Indies about 6 P.M. Almost all over Europe, including Scandinavia, the water in rivers, canals, lakes, and ponds and springs was seen to be suddenly disturbed or to rise and fall in an abnormal manner.

But the attention of the whole of the relevant civilized world was focused on the ruined capital of Portugal. Lisbon is not an easy place to describe to those who have

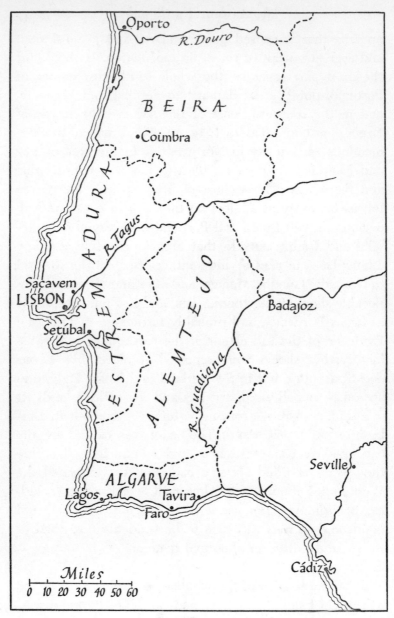

Fig. 1. The earthquake area: Portugal

Fig. 2. The earthquake area: Peninsula and North Africa

never seen the city, and an uncontoured map is a poor guide; for, apart from a fine broad axis of level or gently sloping ground, Lisbon is bumpily and abruptly hilly, so much so that the extremely steep slopes that sometimes face the visitor when trying to make his way from the lower city either to the east or to the west are among the town's unforgettable features. The Cidade Baixa is, however, flat from the Tagus shore to the top of the Rossio Square, and beyond this the Avenida, running in a south-east to north-west direction from the Restauradores, rises gradually towards the Praça do Pombal and the Parque Eduardo VII, which leads up to a level ridge of much higher ground; but on each side of the Cidade Baixa are tall cliffs of houses and gardens, bordering the hilly lateral districts, Lisboa oriental and Lisboa occidental, which are themselves broken up into steep-sided promontories, small plateaus, and deep valleys, so that Lisbon, seen from its famous *miradouros* (viewpoints), such as the Castle or Graça on the eastern heights, or the Alameda de São Pedro de Alcântara on the western ridge, appears as a city with a low-lying central area that is set in an encompassing cup-like frame of broken hilly country, now as crowded with buildings as the lower town itself.

Lisbon was not, before the earthquake, a city of great architectural beauty in plan or style, and apart from a large open space by the river, flanked by the Royal Palace (Pl. II) and government buildings, it must have had a jumbled partly medieval appearance, very pleasant with its handsome water-front with biggish ships in dock almost under the palace windows, and rising behind this great square an agreeable forest of towers and spires, evidence of the fact that most of the important buildings in Lisbon were churches or convents. It was not a very large city, but it had over forty parish churches, several non-parochial churches, and about ninety convents. Writing twenty-five years before the great earthquake, a French observer said it was dirty and not lit at night, but his picture is nevertheless of a charming city; for he found much to admire. Not only the palaces and churches; he said the fish-market was the best in the world, and the meat-market, he observed, was spotlessly clean and lined with the famous *azulejos* (glazed tiles) of the country; both these two buildings were on the front, the meat-market in the palace square, the Terreiro do Paço. He observed that the chief building material used in the palaces and bigger houses was a marble that cracked a great deal and had often to be patched up with mastic; this pretty pinkish stone can still be seen in quantities, for in spite of its cracks it is very good building material.

Appearance apart, the most important thing about Lisbon was that it was staggeringly rich, rich in the almost fabulous contents of its palaces and churches, rich in the great stores of bullion and jewels and costly merchandise in its wharves and business premises, rich in its tremendous commercial importance. Portugal, the country, was not rich: for its finances were badly run and the extravagances of João V (1706-50) were of the kind that would exhaust even Eldorado; moreover, the very powerful British Factory in Lisbon had a grip on Portuguese commerce and Brazilian gold that the Portuguese had already begun to resent. But Lisbon itself was justly famous for its wealth, and because of its commercial activity it was one of the best-known cities in the world. Protestant visitors and traders, particularly the English and the Germans who did most of the business in the town, also knew Lisbon as a city of the Inquisition, and this influential section of the outside world knew much more about autos-da-fé in Lisbon than in Spain; they also knew a great deal about what was called the superstitious idolatry of the Lisbon people. Wealth, the Inquisition, and the worship of images: to an appreciably large section of the

outside world Lisbon was famous for these three things.
Other Latin countries were not likely to object to the
exuberant religious observances of devout Portuguese; but
the Portuguese were not on very good terms with France,
were traditionally suspicious of Spain, and not unreserv-
edly devoted to the Vatican. At the time of the earthquake Portugal was an aloof, proud, happy, spendthrift
country, forced to buy things that it should itself have
produced, and slipping fast into financial dependence on
London and Hamburg.

The amount of damage done to Lisbon by the earthquake on 1 November was very great. Some of the finest
buildings in the city were in the greater part ruined and
hundreds of the smaller houses and shops were completely
destroyed. Observers in ships on the Tagus and on the
higher ground round Lisbon talk about the city seeming
to sway like corn in the wind before the avalanches of
descending masonry hid the ruins under a cloud of dust.
In the huge basilica, São Vicente de Fora, the priests in
the choir, on reaching the words of the introit *Gaudeamus
omnes in Deo,* said that they felt the great grey marble
church suddenly rock and sway like an unsteady ship at
sea.

The area of severe shock that included Lisbon, as
mapped by Pereira de Sousa (*see* Bibliography, p. 247),
extended along the north shore of the Tagus at the Lisbon bend from a point close to the present Santos station on the Cascais line to Braço de Prata, half-way between Lisbon and Sácavem, and is a belt of country six
or seven miles long extending inland to a depth of about
one and a half miles. Inside this area there were dis-

tricts in which the shocks were of greater intensity and did more damage than elsewhere. Pereira de Sousa used a modified Mercalli scale in order to measure the effects of the earthquake. IX denotes bad damage, churches wrecked but repairable, houses totally ruined or rendered uninhabitable, and casualties light; X represents very bad damage, churches so ruined that they had to be completely rebuilt, cracked ground and landslides, and heavy casualties. He was thus able to give a useful, though only approximate, indication of the state of affairs in Lisbon. It seems that damage was very severe (X) all along the Tagus shore from (using modern landmarks) the Praça de D. Luis and the Cais do Sodré to the Museu de Artilharia; the western boundary of this heavy damage lay along the north-south line of the Rua de O Século that descends from the little plateau of the Praça do Principe Real, rises up to the parish church of Nossa Senhora das Mercês, which was not seriously ruined, and then goes down into the Calçada do Combro, across which the line continues up the steps to the Santa Catarina hill and then down to the shore west of the old Mint, a building that also escaped heavy damage. The central area of devastation on this same scale (X) extended in a north-south direction from the top of Rossio to the Tagus, westwards nearly to the line of the Rua do Alecrim and the Rua da Misericordia, and eastwards to the Rua dos Douradores.

In eastern Lisbon there were two areas of major ruin, one the castle hill and its southern slopes as far as the Igreja da Sé (the Cathedral, then known as the Basilica de Santa Maria) and then down the hill to the Cais de Santarém; the other the high ground on which stand Graça and São Vicente de Fora with its southern and eastern slopes. The earthquake was also felt on this same heavy scale round the Campo dos Mártires, and farther to the north-east on the hill of Nossa Senhora de Penha de França.

The damage was on the lower scale (IX) on the western slope of the Castle hill above the Rua da Madalena in a belt that curves round eastwards past and including the Sé[1] and down to the Igreja da Conceicão Velha, which preserves the elaborate Manueline (sixteenth century) portico of the wrecked Misericordia Church formerly on the site. The damage was also less severe on the east slope of the Castle hill, where much of the Alfama district to a great extent escaped both earthquake and fire. In western Lisbon there was another area marked at scale IX which ran southwards from São Roque, including the Rua da Misericordia, the Praça de Camões, and the Rua de Alecrim.

The fire greatly increased the destruction begun by the earthquake. The Royal Palace and the magnificent new Opera House, completed in March of this same year, many of the government offices, and the fantastically splendid Patriarchal Church, might all have survived with not a great deal of harm done if the fire had not consumed them, and this is also true of many other notable buildings and churches; but subsequent disaster does not alter the fact that the earthquake alone did enormous

---

[1] The engraving by Le Bas of the Igreja da Sé after the earthquake shows an almost complete ruin, but these prints (see Pl. IV) are untrustworthy, and Pereira de Sousa thought that structurally it was not so seriously wrecked as this picture suggests; he therefore includes the Sé in a Scale IX area. The Cathedral was burnt out in the fire, and the conflicting accounts of what actually happened to this building on 1 November 1755 show how difficult it is to measure the effect of the earthquake on that day by a modern scale of seismic intensity.

damage and killed a tragically large number of people. Over twenty parish churches were ruined; many palaces and fine houses, and some of the largest convents were wrecked before the fire completed their destruction; the home of the Inquisition at the top of the Rossio Square was tumbled to the ground; the Castle and Santa Cruz do Castelo suffered heavily. But the earthquake's main damage was done to the ordinary houses and the rows of shops. Right through central Lisbon and on the flanking slopes these lesser buildings were for the most part shattered beyond recovery.

This terrible fire, fanned by a north-east wind, burnt strongly and was not finally extinguished until nearly a week after the earthquake; it gutted the whole of the central, low-lying part of the city and also much of the town on the adjacent hill-slopes. The contemporary accounts say it started almost at once in various parts of the ruins, for example in the Carmo and the Trindade convents, and also in the palace of the Marquês de Louriçal in the Largo da Anunciada on the east side of the Avenida; but it quickly became a general conflagration, spreading from the top of Rossio towards the river, and also over the western and southern slopes of the Castle hill, and, on the other side of the Cidade Baixa, right over the Carmo ridge down to the Rua do Alecrim and beyond this up to the top of the hill on which stands the Chagas Church. Taking a line along the shore of about a mile from the Church of São Paulo near the Cais do Sodré station to the east end of the Rua Cais de Santarem, the fire burnt up the whole of central Lisbon north of it, on the west up to, though not including, São Roque, in the centre up to the top of Rossio, and on the east right up to the southern wards of the Castle (cf. Pl. V). It was as savage a gutting of the heart of a city as can be found anywhere in the previous history of Europe, and after this ferocious blaze had done its work the richest and most thickly populated district of Lisbon was a charred desert of smoking ruins with the dead bodies of hundreds of the inhabitants lying beneath the ashes and cinders of their homes.

It was this fire that led to the heaviest loss of the city's material wealth, much of which might otherwise have been recovered from the earthquake ruins; but the flames spared little or nothing of the pictures, furniture, tapestries, and plate in the churches and in the palaces and great houses, or of the great libraries, or of the vast stocks of merchandise in the shops, where the losses of jewellery, plate, and silks were said to be, and no doubt were, enormous. Some of the merchants in the Rua Nova dos Mercadores and the Rua da Confeitaria dragged what they could of their goods out of their wrecked premises after the earthquake and began to organize salvage dumps in the Terreiro do Paço, but later on the fire reached the great square and burnt the whole lot. The losses in goods suffered by the foreign traders were estimated at 48,000,-000 Spanish dollars (about £12,000,000 sterling), of which 32,000,000 was the British share; next in the list come the Hamburg merchants whose losses were estimated at 8,000,000 dollars.

The palace of the Marquês de Louriçal stood well clear to the north of the main area of the fire; but the rich contents of his home, all destroyed, show the kind of thing this loss of property meant: two hundred pictures, including works by Titian, Correggio and Rubens, a library of eighteen thousand printed books, one thousand manuscripts, including a history written by the Emperor Charles V in his own hand, a herbal formerly belonging to King Matthias Hunyadi (1440-90) of Hungary, a huge family archive, and a great collection of maps and charts relating to the Portuguese voyages of discovery and colonization in the East and in the New World. It is said that seventy thousand books perished in the burning of the King's palace in the north-west corner of the present Terreiro do Paço; the Bragança archive was burnt in the Palacio dos Duques de Bragança at the bottom of the Rua Antonio Maria Cordoso, and a valuable library of Marian literature, including many incunables, was destroyed in the Oratory on the site of the Grandes Armazens at the east end of the Chiado at the crossing of the Rua do Carmo and the Rua Nova do Almada; the fire also burnt another fine library, carefully catalogued and open for public use, in the convent of the Dominicans at the north-east corner of the Rossio Square.

All descriptions of the earthquake by those who were near the shore or in boats on the Tagus tell with horror of the great waves that suddenly came pouring over the north shore at about eleven o'clock; for ships were torn from their anchors, crashed against each other and against the quays, and all the light shore structures were washed away. The seismic waves started out at sea and, coming in towards Lisbon from the south-west, were to some extent resisted at the river bar; but even so they were formidable enough, fifteen to twenty feet high, it was said, and three times they flung themselves at the whole six miles of river-coast from Lisbon to the mouth of the Tagus, as also along the south-facing coast to Cascais and

Cabo Raso, and against the west coast at least as far as Ericeira. It seems, however, that in their fullest violence they struck against the low-lying São Paulo district of Lisbon and the Terreiro do Paço, and here their force was such that they greatly damaged the Alfándega buildings (Customs House) and completed the destruction of the fine marble-faced Cais de Pedra in front of the Alfándega, a magnificent new quay built by João V, the stones of which had already been loosened and partly dislodged by the earthquake.[2] Here a large number of people, probably over a hundred, who had taken refuge on what seemed to be a safe open place convenient for escape across the river, were washed away and drowned, as many other people were drowned up and down the coast. The waters, however, had spent their force with the third wave, and gradually the river became quiet. Boats had begun again to cross the Tagus with refugees by about two o'clock in the afternoon.

No one will ever know the number of people who lost their lives in the Lisbon earthquake. First accounts understandably gave wildly exaggerated estimates, and it was extremely difficult to replace the early guesses by convincing official statistics. The confusion caused by the frantic evacuation of the ruined area of the city made an immediate worth-while roll-call impossible, for nobody could tell whether a missing person was lying dead under the rubble or had escaped into the suburbs or the

[2] The commonly repeated story that the Cais de Pedra was suddenly swallowed up in an earthquake chasm was disproved by Portuguese engineers shortly after the earthquake. See Moreira de Mendonça, *Historia Universal dos Terremotos,* p. 134, and for modern opinion on this point, Harry Fielding Reid, *Bull. Seismological Society of America,* iv, 2 (June 1914), pp. 54-55.

country; there was no means of ascertaining the numbers of lodgers and strangers in the town, and most of the civic records on which some sort of census could be based had been burnt. The first attempt to count the casualties was a questionnaire sent out to the parish priests throughout the country, but the returns are only available for certain country districts, and those for Lisbon, now missing, are said to have been made too soon; for there had not been time to trace refugees and to let the people settle down in the camps on the outskirts of the ruins so that they could be asked about the fate of their families and their friends. What seem to be the best and most careful estimates agree that probably between ten thousand to fifteen thousand people lost their lives in Lisbon out of a population in the neighbourhood of 275,000, and a very sensible historian of the earthquake, Joachim José Moreira de Mendonça, thought that not more than five thousand people were killed on 1 November, the casualties being doubled or trebled during the course of the month. A large number of the inmates, it is said as many as four hundred, were burnt to death in the Hospital Real, and a great many were killed in the churches, not only because of the big attendances at the morning Masses on All Saints' Day, but because those that were not completely ruined were used for sheltering the wounded and as places of refuge before they were burnt out.

The figures given in many accounts and often quoted are not accurate, but some of the estimates are a measure of the terror of the day. It was said that not one hundred but nine hundred people lost their lives when the great waves poured down on the Cais de Pedra and the Alfándega do Jardim do Tabaco behind it in the Terreiro do

Paço; six hundred people are said to have been crushed to death in the church of the Franciscan convent and twenty of the monks; four hundred were reported to have been killed in the church of the Convento de Santa Trindade; three hundred out of eight hundred morning communicants were believed to have died in the church of the Convento de Nossa Senhora da Penha de França, and 137 people were burnt to death in the parish church of Santa Maria Madalena. The last figure is probably correct, the others guesses that may be in need of wholesale cutting. A statement, for instance, that two hundred people perished in the Oratory was quickly corrected to fifty by one of the Fathers (*see* p. 91): the dreadful events in the parish church of São Paulo killed by earthquake and fire about a hundred persons, and not six hundred, as rumour said. But the earthquake was horrible and indiscriminately murderous; thousands of people were killed by the collapsing city and hundreds were burnt to death in the ghastly conflagration that followed.

Of the swarming population of monks, friars, and nuns in Lisbon about two hundred were killed in the earthquake. There was no very serious loss of life among the foreign commercial population in Lisbon. The British Factory did not lose many of its members, and the total British killed, including some unfortunate casualties of whom almost nothing was known but their names, came to seventy-seven. Of these forty-nine were women. There were very few casualties among the Portuguese nobility and persons of distinction, probably less than twenty in all, and in the whole of this great disaster that struck so hard at Portugal and Spain only two deaths have become memorable, in Lisbon that of the Spanish Ambassador, the Conde de Peralda, who was killed escaping from the front door of his embassy, and, in Cádiz, that of the young Racine, great-grandson of the famous dramatist.

The descriptions of the misery and suffering of the unhappy people of Lisbon on 1 November and the following days are the common tales told of such disasters; but they do not seem less terrible because of that. There are accounts of folk creeping out of the wreckage, bleeding and with broken limbs, stumbling about in search of the rest of their family, of cries for help, of screaming children, and of the frantic agonies of the wounded animals, mules, horses, and dogs; of suicidal attempts to escape from the upper stories of partly wrecked houses; of obstinate people who could not be persuaded to seek safety and had to be abandoned; of little groups of terrified people forming together and setting off on aimless expeditions, turning about whenever some rumour of a safe place reached them or whenever they were threatened by fire or collapsing walls; tales of bolting into churches, dossing down in the squares, and also of the great persistent exodus to the open country. Tales also of great bravery and resignation shown by the sufferers.

The first night after the earthquake was terrible, for now the roaring flames had a firm grip on the town, and there was still a pitiful background noise of groans and cries and the howling of dogs. The dreadful waves had done terrible damage, and no one knew whether it was safe to be near the river; fires and crashing walls were blocking some of the main roads leading to the country; most of the narrow lanes, alleys, and steps between the buildings on the hill-slopes were impassable; thieves and galley slaves had escaped from the prisons and already started robbing the dead and wounded, and plundering in the ruins; a rumour that the powder magazine in the Castle was at any minute likely to blow up, which had been widely spread during the day, was still tormenting those who knew of the possibility. The scenes in the big squares, especially Rossio and the Terreiro do Paço, must have been truly appalling. In Rossio the palace of the Inquisition, São Domingos and the adjacent Ermida of Nossa Senhora de Escada were in ruins, and fires were still burning [3] on all sides and in the skeletons of the great convents on the western hill; the roads leading out of it from the south side were choked with ruins and smashed traffic; and in the square the miserable sick inmates of the burning Hospital Real had been dumped down, exposed and helpless, while little groups of the refugees from the surrounding buildings camped there with their wounded in discomfort and dread. And among them all the time moved priests, confessing and giving absolution.[4] Of all the horrors of the Lisbon earthquake no horror was worse than the supreme terror of dying unconfessed and unforgiven.

The great exodus from the central area of the city began at once, and was joined by crowds of people from the built-up areas on the perimeter of the wrecked part

[3] The fires in São Domingos and the hospital were at their height about 3 P.M.

[4] This caused alarm to one or two Protestant casualties. The miserable young Mr. Chase, aet. 26, helpless from his injuries, was in the Terreiro do Paço, and at the approach of priests pretended to be unconscious in case the zealous papists might deem it meritorious to burn a heretic in the approaching flames. One English clergyman, unable to speak Portuguese, found himself hemmed in by a crowd and baptized by Portuguese priests.

of the town. It was in part a sensible and in part a disgraceful flight. The contemporary accounts of the earthquake say bluntly that there was a desperate scramble to get out of Lisbon by frightened mobs of hysterical people, clutching crucifixes and images of saints, and bits and scraps of their belongings, all trying to reach open country. Almost every section of the population was represented among the refugees. For example the greater part of the garrison of the Casa da Moeda (the Mint) near the Cais do Sodré, in which was a big store of newly arrived gold from Brazil, joined in the flight, only a young lieutenant and four soldiers having the courage to remain at their posts and protect the building as best they could from fire and from robbers. Many writers have described the terrified streams of people trying to get away from Lisbon and the misery and suffering of the flight. Our example here, however, shall be the comparatively unsensational adventures of Father Manuel Portal of the Oratory, quoted from a manuscript source by Pereira de Sousa.

For this holy man the day of 1 November began unhappily as he had had a bad dream during the night, in which, he says, there were two earthquake shocks, noticed also by other people. He awoke greatly distressed, for he had been warned in his dream that he would never see again the beloved crucifix on the wall of his cell, and he attended Mass in a state of penitent alarm. Then came the great earthquake, and he found himself partly buried in the wreckage of one of the corridors of the convent; eventually he was with some difficulty extricated by his comrades, and when he was set free, though he was badly injured as one of his legs had been crushed, he did his

of some sort was made for him, but he had to give this up to another Father and camp under a tree. Eventually he was discovered by friends and removed to a hut in the southern part of the *quinta,* where the wretched man remained for some days, very ill and in great discomfort.

The Cidade Baixa was not deserted, though few people dared to live in the houses that were still serviceable as dwellings. Some, however, refused to leave the neighbourhood of their destroyed houses and places of business, and some were too poor to afford to build a hut and live in the suburban camps; the parish priests stuck to their posts, and some members of the religious orders insisted on staying on in the ruins of their convents; moreover, useful men were soon made to return to the destroyed part of the town, particularly technicians and craftsmen who could help in the work of reconstruction. Rossio, Terreiro do Paço, and the Praça da Ribeira were crowded with temporary offices and shops, and there was a constant coming and going of the military called in to maintain order and help with the burying of the dead, and also of engineers and government officials. Stalls were set up for selling food and other necessities, and a town life of a kind went on. But the population had to a considerable extent shifted, and there were now strange new settlements in the open spaces east and west of the destroyed area, and on the high ground encircling the city. The Oratory *quinta* at Cotovia, to which Manuel Portal had escaped, and the surrounding properties formed one of these encampments, and the parish of Santa Isabel in which it was situated is said to have had a refugee population of twenty-five thousand.[6] The Campo de Ourique, the Campo de Santa Ana, the Campo Grande, the Campo Pequeno, and the Campo de Santa Barbara in the Castle, were also filled by little towns of tents and huts; so also the Estrela district in the west and the Campo de Santa Clara on the east side of the town were full of squatters. Right away to the west there were large encampments around Nossa Senhora da Ajuda and at Belém. It was estimated that about nine thousand wooden buildings were put up during the first six months after the quake, a fine achievement, for wood was very scarce indeed in Lisbon and much of it had to be brought to the city for this special purpose.

The King and the royal family were staying, when the earthquake happened, at a royal residence in Belém, but they moved at once into a suite of tents in an open space close at hand, and there they stayed for nine months until a big quadrangular wooden lodging, with twenty-five windows a side, had been erected for them on the Ajuda hill, north of Belém where the great stone palace, built in the early nineteenth century, now stands. His minister Pombal (*see* p. 73) had a hutment lodging at Belém while the King was there; but he probably made use also of his house in the Rua de O Século near the parish church of Nossa Senhora das Mercês, which, though on the fringe of a badly ruined area, seems to have been more or less undamaged.[7] The general desire was to get out of buildings into tents or huts, and to sleep in the garden rather than indoors, even if one's home still stood safe and

[6] Matos Sequeira, *Depois do Terremoto,* I, 32, reduces the figure to "more than 6,000."

[7] Pombal had also some newly built property in the parish of São Julião in the Cidade Baixa that escaped damage.

sound, and for this reason the great camps on the high
and open places round the city were for a long time
crowded communities, in spite of the initial discomfort
and squalor of the miserable bivouacs of matting, planks,
and sail-cloth under which many of the squatters spent
their first few nights.

The most remarkable concourse of these campers was
that in and around the *quinta* of the Oratory in Cotovia.
The company included the Patriarch and his staff, some
members of the nobility, and a number of nuns from the
ruined Convento das Trinas do Rato which was close to
the present Praça do Rato. The farm and vineyards of
the *quinta* suffered badly, but in a little while an ordered
settlement of wooden huts was established, and some of
these, built for nobles and high officials, began to be quite
luxurious bungalows with glass windows and tapestry
hangings and good domestic offices. The Patriarch built
a properly furnished chapel, and the Oratory also built
themselves decent wooden premises with a small church.
The Patriarch made a daily distribution of food and en-
tertained charitably on a very large scale. The clergy
from the Patriarchal Church had been transferred to the
Ermida of São Joaquim and Santa Anna in Alcântara; but
they were frightened out of this by an earthquake on 21
December; later on a very grand wooden church was
made for them on what had been the Conde de Tarouca's
property on the side of the road leading from São Roque
to the Rato. The Patriarch himself, after a year in the
quinta of the Oratory, moved into the palace of the lately
disgraced minister Diogo de Mendonça Côrte Real. The
Marquês de Louriçal, whose town palace had been burnt,
also built a fine wooden house in this neighbourhood on

the Estrada do Rato, and before long most of the rich people in temporary lodgings were as comfortable as they could be under such circumstances and were behaving in an ostentatiously gay and cheerful manner. In fact, they were considered to be a little too high-spirited. The ladies began to go about in their prettiest and most expensive clothes, and in February 1756 the Patriarch thought it proper to correct this ostentation by forbidding them to wear coloured hats in church in place of the customary dark veils.

It was inevitable that some imperturbable folk should begin to joke about the whole adventure, and mock in private the superstitious fears of the majority, for it seemed that God was persistently flouting the prayers of his devoted Portuguese worshippers; but that was not the common mood, and throughout Lisbon there was still a mood of anxiety. The dreadful thing was that the earthquakes continued. They were mostly brief after-shocks that did no damage, but they kept hysterical fright alive and seemed to justify the predictions of the numerous prophets of woe who said that God had not yet completed the punishment of the sinful city of Lisbon. It was alleged that there were nearly thirty earthquake shocks in the week after 1 November, and before the end of the year there were certainly some that caused very great alarm, a violent shock at 5:30 A.M. on 8 November, three more shocks in the middle of the month, and a really thunderous quake, causing panic and evacuation, in the early morning of 11 December. There was another earthquake that caused excessive alarm on 21 December. "Will your Earth never be quiet?" asked Sir Benjamin Keene, the British Ambassador in Madrid, on

31 July 1756, in a letter to Castres, British Envoy in Lisbon. In August 1756 it was said that there had been five hundred after-shocks since the dreadful day of 1 November 1755. No wonder most of the Lisbon people remained wretchedly apprehensive; no wonder vehement orators pursued them with exhortations, scoldings, and threats; no wonder they believed that the anger of God against Lisbon had not been turned aside. Where was it all to stop? Who could find safety? What other sinful community was God going to punish next? No wonder that the clergy of many nations had to go up into their pulpits and answer as best they could the question that their suddenly serious congregations now asked in conscience-stricken alarm, "Wherefore hath the Lord done thus unto this great city?"

Chapter Three

MEN OF ACTION AND
MEN OF SCIENCE

In his sensible little *Commentary* [1] on the Lisbon earthquake published in 1756, António Pereira of the Oratory (afterwards António Pereira de Figueiredo) mentioned four people who had greatly contributed to the restoration of order and confidence after the disaster. Monsenhor Sampaio of the Patriarchal Church, who worked so hard at burying dead bodies that he is believed to have assisted personally at the interment of 240 people; Dom João de Bragança, cousin of the King and younger brother of the Duque de Lafões, who distinguished himself in the rescue work without any regard to his own safety; the Duque de Lafões himself, who did so much to preserve order and prevent looting, tirelessly devoting himself to his duties and neglecting sleep and meals in order to get on with his task; and finally the aged Patriarch, Cardinal José Manuel (1686-1758), who did his best to arrange that his clergy could continue to perform their spiritual and practical tasks. In 1758 in his much fuller account [2] of the earthquake, Joachim José

---

[1] p. 90 *infra*. [2] p. 247 *infra*.

Moreira de Mendonça praised the same four distinguished people, mentioned the signal generosity of the three Palhavã princes, illegitimate sons of João V,[3] and the admirable handling of the earthquake-crisis in general by King José, assisted by his Secretary of State, Sebastião José de Carvalho e Mello, a wise and active minister.

In 1764 there was published a little potted history of all that had happened in Lisbon from the earthquake to the expulsion of the Jesuits,[4] also by António Pereira de Figueiredo, and in it we read that everything written, ordered, or done in the name of His Most Faithful Majesty in respect of burying the dead, restoring morale, collecting provisions, calling in troops, dealing with looting, providing protection against African pirates, stopping and controlling refugees, maintaining a strict military discipline, protecting nuns, averting God's wrath, preserving the King's person, punishing traitors, suppressing Jesuits, restoring commerce, encouraging the arts, clearing the ruins, planning and rebuilding the city, all this, we are told, was in the greater part due to the foresight, wisdom, and authority of the Conde de Oeiras. The Conde de Oeiras was the new title, created in 1759, of Sebastião José de Carvalho e Mello, the future Marquês de Pombal, a title conferred on him in 1770 (Pl. VI).

That was the proper way to write about a great dic-

[3] *Os meninos de Palhavã*, so called because they were brought up in the Palhavã palace, now the Spanish embassy, north of the city, close to the present Feira Popular on the Benfica road. They were officially recognized by King José as his brothers at the beginning of the earthquake year.

[4] *Rerum Lusitanarum Ephemerides . . .*, Lisbon, 1761. And *Diário dos successos de Lisboa desde o terremoto até o exterminio dos Jezuitas.* Traduzido do idiom a Latino por Mathias Pereira de Azevedo Pinto, Lisbon, 1766.

tator such as Pombal had by then become. He towered above everybody else in ability and authority, and nobody could any longer approach him in any distribution of credit. After a due lip-service to the King, he took it all. Moreover, some of those praised in 1756 for their distinguished services in the earthquake-crisis had disappeared. The Patriarch, José Manuel, and the first Duque de Lafões were dead. Pombal had exiled Dom João of Bragança, second Duke of Lafões, who, after being made F.R.S. in London in 1757, was now in Austria; he had disgraced the two Palhavã princes, António and José, and the third, Gaspar, the Archbishop of Braga, was living in a state of toadying apprehension. The dictator stood alone as the earthquake-hero.

Pombal was born in 1699. His career as Dictator of Portugal lasted throughout the whole of the reign of José I, who became King in 1750 and died in 1777, and is a brilliant, startling, and sometimes lamentable and terrifying, chapter in the history of his country. When King José died his famous minister was disgraced and ended his days in exile in 1782 in a house in the market-square of the little town of Pombal between Coimbra and Leiria, from which he took his title. He was the son of a simple country squire, and though he was from the beginning a thruster, he was also a troublesome and touchy person, and he did not make any substantial advance in politics until he was thirty-nine years old. He owed his first connexions with the court to an uncle who was an official in the Patriarchal Church, but his career really began with his marriage to the widow of a nobleman and niece of the Conde de Arcos, a match strongly opposed by the bride's family. Having inherited money and now attained a social position, he lived bravely and showily, aided in his political ambitions by an important relative, eleven years his senior, Marc António de Azevedo Coutinho (1688-1750), whom in 1739 he succeeded as Minister Plenipotentiary in London. In 1745 he was sent on a mission to Vienna, where his first wife having died, he made another splendid match by marrying an Austrian lady of famous lineage, a union that was a lifelong happiness to him and also one that greatly increased his prestige in the Portuguese court, for Queen Maria Ana was an Austrian. He was still a climbing man, financially ruined because of his heavy Vienna expenses and angry at the loss of his London appointment as he had wanted to return to England to recover his losses; but when he was back in Portugal in 1749 he found he had two powerful friends in the Queen Regent, for João V was dying, and Coutinho, now Secretary of State, and on the accession of José I he obtained a post in the Cabinet as Minister for Foreign Affairs and War. Very quickly he established himself as the dominant figure in Portuguese politics, and as quickly he made himself hated by a jealous group of noblemen whose prestige he flouted and whose formidable influence he had already begun to undermine. Then came the earthquake.

The obsequious paragraph in António Pereira's little history of 1761 comes near enough to being a fair tribute to a man of exceptional ability, for there is so much to be said against Pombal, that this one thing at least should be left indisputably to his credit, namely that his bravery and common sense rescued ruined Lisbon, inspired its citizens with the courage that resolute leadership can give, and in a large measure prevented his country from suffering an appalling economic and social disaster. He was in undisputed command from the day of the earthquake, and letters and dispatches written in Lisbon in the following days by foreigners reporting the terrible events contain sincere and admiring tributes to Senhor de Carvalho's firm handling of the situation. It is a well-known story that when the unhappy young King (José was thirty-six) in his first misery on learning the dreadful nature of the catastrophe asked despairingly what was to be done, Pombal replied: "Bury the dead and feed the living." It is an apocryphal saying, and in anti-Pombal literature is attributed to the Duque de Aveiro or the Marquês de Alorna; but it is so likely to be in some near form what Pombal really did say, so succinctly expresses the practical measures he at once caused to be carried out, that it has rightly become immortal as a classic example of the blunt common sense of a man of action breaking roughly and abruptly through another man's mood of dithering emotional helplessness.

In 1758 a handsome folio volume was published [5] in Lisbon containing the principal directives whereby Senhor de Carvalho had controlled the earthquake emergency and had restored order and confidence in Lisbon and throughout Portugal. It is fulsomely dedicated to King José, who is extolled as the immensely brave and immensely wise saviour of his country, and it is a mag-

[5] *Memorias das principaes Providencias que se derão no Terremoto, que padeceo a Corte de Lisboa no anno de 1775* . . . por Amador Patricio de Lisboa. The author is said to be Francisco José Freire (1719-73), later a distinguished poet and literary man, and, like António Pereira, a member of the Oratory; both were in the Convento do Espirito Santo at the time of the earthquake.

nificent book, of which Portugal may justly be proud; but
the compiler remained discreetly anonymous, and it is
really a monument to Pombal by Pombal, as noble as
the big bronze medallion of himself that he caused to be
fixed on the plinth of the great equestrian statue of King
José in the Terreiro do Paço, which he unveiled in 1775,[6]
and as showy and impressive as the great twentieth-century marble monument to the dictator that now domi-
nates the Avenida from its central position in the Praça
do Pombal. Politically, Pombal did need a monument as
early as 1758, for enemies, jealous of his power, had already begun to intrigue against him, and even his meritorious services at the time of the earthquake, of which
in this book he pointedly reminded the Portuguese, even
these had not erased the detestation with which his quick
climb to power and the brutal ruthlessness of his methods
of doing so were regarded by many of the nobles, while
the Jesuits had already good reason for using their influence in every possible way against him. But, even with
this discreditable background, and in spite of the anti-
Pombal judgement that his earthquake-administration was
a series of belated measures desperately following a situation beyond his control, no impartial person can read
the *Providencias* without a warm respect for the strong
realistic administration whereby Pombal did deal firmly
with conditions dangerously liable to degenerate into a
state of lawless panic. In a clearly expressed and consistent series of documents, beginning on the day of the
earthquake itself, Pombal is revealed handling with un-

[6] The medallion was removed after Pombal's disgrace and the intention was to destroy it; but the artist hid it and handed on the secret of
its whereabouts, so that it was possible for a Liberal government to replace it in 1833.

ruffled determination one after another of the anxieties
and crises inevitably attending a major disaster of this
kind.

Nevertheless, it was really the Portuguese people who
saved the situation, for the best of them behaved bravely
and performed their duties calmly in the dangerous days
of November 1755. Pombal could have achieved little in
the earthquake-crisis if he had not been strongly and will-
ingly supported, and a complete account of the events
after the disaster would give credit to the invaluable services of many of the Portuguese whose parts in this agonizing drama may now seem to be only minor roles sup-
porting the dominant performance of the chief actor.
First, Dom Pedro de Bragança, Duque de Lafões (1718-
61), the Chief Justice, who was responsible for the civil
government of the kingdom; next, the third Marquês de
Marialva, Dom Diogo de Noronha (1688-1761), Grand
Master of the Horse, and responsible for the military government; then, Fernão Telles da Silva, Marquês de Ale-
grete, Monteiro-Mór (King's Huntsman), President of the
Senate, and responsible for the economic administration; [7]
the second Marquês de Abrantes, Commander-in-Chief,
and many other high-ranking officers of the forces; then
the members of the able and active Câmara Municipal in
Lisbon, who presided jealously over the interests of the
citizens, even if it was necessary to oppose or criticize
Pombal's measures; then the specially appointed magistrates of the twelve *bairros*, and the engineers and sur-
veyors headed by Manuel de Maia (1680-1768), chief
engineer and officer-in-charge of the Torre do Tombo,

[7] The first three names are somewhat coldly mentioned as the principal executive officials in the *Providencias*, pp. 39-40.

Carlos Mardel, a senior engineer, and Eugénio dos Santos, names best known during the subsequent planning and building of the new Lisbon, though each did work which was as valuable in the first and worst days of the crisis. All these men, and there were many others, can be identified in action through the directives addressed to them; but there must have been also a heroic company of folk whose names do not figure with deserved emphasis in the contemporary accounts of the earthquake.

The part played by the Church does require proper honour because later events have, with some reason, made Pombal appear in history as a violently anti-clerical statesman who in the earthquake-period was driven to exasperation by the obstruction and non-coöperation of certain sections of the Lisbon clergy. We shall see in later chapters how bitter, and how understandable, was the conflict between him and the preachers who in his view exploited the earthquake in an alarmist and anti-social manner; but that quarrel must not spoil a tribute to the general body of the clergy whose conduct immediately after the earthquake was both helpful and heroic.

The Cardinal Patriarch's conscientious direction of the Church has been fairly recorded, and also the magnificent work of the religious orders, particularly the Oratory Fathers, the Jesuits, the Benedictines, and the Austin Friars; but insufficient tribute has been paid to the ordinary parish priests of the worst-damaged area of the city; for no one reading the earthquake-accounts can fail to be impressed by the bravery and devotion of these men who remained at their posts in conditions of great danger and terrifying confusion. They did their best to carry on their parochial duties in whatever makeshift ac-

commodation they could contrive as close as possible to
the ruins of their churches, and in huts and tents right
among the ruins and the fires they stayed on duty where
their people could find them and where in some form
or other the accustomed worship could be maintained.
They were present to act as the main agents in estab-
lishing a roll-call after the disaster and to deal with the
official inquiries about their surviving parishioners, the
casualties, the number of the folk who had fled from
the town. The action of these brave men is only briefly
recorded, but in most cases their emergency measures are
known. For example, the *pároco* of São Julião moved into
the Terreiro do Paço and worked there for two years in
a wooden cabin which for a time he shared with the
parish priest of the burnt-out Santa Maria Madalena; the
parishes of SS. Justa and Rufina and of São Nicolau had
their headquarters in huts in the Rossio Square, where
the Inquisition had also set up a temporary wooden office; the *pároco* of the ruined Church of Santo Cruz do
Castello continued his ministry in a hut built in his church-
yard, and the parish priest of the destroyed Church of
São Pedro, south of the Castle hill, used for a time a ware-
house on the river-side as his church.

What Pombal had to do, and succeeded in doing, with
all this strong support is, in brief summary, as follows.
On the day after the earthquake he told the Duque
de Lafões to appoint the special magistrates mentioned
above, one for each of the twelve *bairros* or wards of
the city, with overriding powers for the administration of
their districts in accordance with the government's emergency directions, which he saw to it thereafter descended
upon these officials in a reassuringly ample supply. His

immediate concern was to prevent a plague, and it was imperative to get rid as quickly as possible of all the corpses, human and animal, that lay in the ruins, and to get rid of the pools of stinking, stagnant water. On 2 November, Pombal suggested to the Patriarch that the quickest and safest method of dealing with the human bodies was that they should be collected in barges, towed out beyond the Tagus bar, and then weighed and sunk. The Patriarch agreed immediately [8] to this proposal, and he was subsequently told to order his clergy to do everything they could to get the corpses buried or removed. The remaining civil population also joined in the work, which was to be assisted in every possible way by the troops called to Lisbon.[9] The next urgent matter was that of food supplies. Stores had to be commandeered wherever there were big depots within reach of Lisbon, and there was a rather rough seizing of whole cargoes and of surplus supplies found on the ships in the harbour, even though the cargoes were destined for other countries. Transport, particularly wagons, had also to be requisitioned and some sort of traffic through the ruins established, so that supplies could move freely. Food centres had to be organized and camp-kitchens and ovens

[8] The numerous contemporary Portuguese accounts of the strenuous efforts made in disposing of the dead do not make any reference to the procedure. If it was carried out at all, it was probably done in a way that attracted no public notice.

[9] In August 1756 Caleb Whitefoord said the ruins of the Trindade, in which many people had been killed, stank abominably, and many Portuguese accounts refer to the smell of the corpses. Whitefoord says there was an outbreak of spotted fever, as indeed there may have been; but his description is much exaggerated, e.g. "there are not three houses left entire in all the city of Lisbon. In the suburbs indeed there are a few standing, but they are so rent and shatter'd as not to be inhabitable." *Whitefoord Papers*, pp. 126-31. Oxford, 1898.

constructed; millers, bakers, and cooks had to be prevented from leaving the city and made to get on with
their work as best they could. Prices of foodstuffs had
to be strictly controlled in order to prevent profiteering,
and every vexatious hindrance in the way of a quick food
supply was removed; for instance, the fish from the Tagus
could be sold anywhere on the fifty-mile stretch between
Belém and Santarém free of duty. Another urgent matter was that of the hospital and shelter services for the
wounded and destitute, which had to be rapidly developed and helped by supplies of beds and medical necessities; also prisons and all institutions where there were
helpless people needed inspection and aid.

It was essential to do everything possible to stop looting and robbery at once. No mercy could be shown, and
the immediate public execution after summary trial of
any thief caught in the act was authorized on 4 November. António Pereira says that within a few days of the
earthquake thirty-four people were executed for looting,
eleven Portuguese, ten Spaniards (there were a large
number of Spanish deserters in Lisbon), five Irishmen,
three Savoyards, two Frenchmen, one Pole, one Fleming,
and one Moor. Regional depots under guard were set up
for the storage of valuables deposited by the homeless or
recovered from uninhabited ruins. Householders and merchants were discouraged from attempting the salvage of
lost belongings without carrying with them unimpeach-
able proof of their identity and right to retrieve possessions. Ships had to be searched for escaped criminals, and
all small river traffic watched carefully and permitted to
move under a licence valid for a day only; the crews of
the bigger ships were not allowed ashore, and the ves-

sels themselves not allowed to leave the Tagus until crews and cargoes had been examined by Portuguese officials. For a long time the most strict disciplinary control was necessary; in February 1756 the Patriarch had to threaten with excommunication persons of either sex who were caught masquerading as monks and nuns in order to obtain alms and assistance under false pretences, and almost a year after the earthquake it was necessary to order the arrest of the people who were going about prophesying that there was going to be another great earthquake on 1 November 1756, for this was done in some cases deliberately in order to make frightened people leave their houses for the open spaces, thus creating conditions in which pillaging was as easy as it was in November 1755.

A particularly difficult problem was the control of the refugees from the city. They were finding their way all over the country, and among them were thieves, escaped prisoners, and rascals of all kinds, in addition to a large number of able-bodied craftsmen and labourers who were needed in Lisbon. A system of passes had to be introduced, and the provincial governors instructed to send back to the capital all those who had escaped to a distance without very good reason.

Another urgent business was the provision of temporary shelter for the homeless and the collection of material for making huts. Profiteering in wood, of which there was a shortage, was stopped, and all available supplies were commandeered for Lisbon. Rents of land used for the erection of emergency hutments were controlled. People were encouraged to return, where possible, to their homes, and landlords were not allowed to evict their tenants from surviving dwelling-houses, and those who kept lodgings were not allowed to put up their prices. Particular attention had to be paid to the protection and housing of homeless and scattered nuns, for the physical distress of many of these holy women and the brutalities to which some of them were subjected, deeply upset and demoralized the ordinary pious folk of the city. The rehousing of the nuns whose convents were destroyed proved in fact to be one of the hardest tasks in the reorganization of Lisbon, for whole communities had to be reassembled and decent accommodation found for them, so that it was many months before the problem was on its way towards solution.

Fire-fighting, with the aid of soldiers hurried into the capital, began at once, as did the clearance of streets and passages through the ruins, the demolition of dangerous structures, and first-aid to buildings still worth saving. Salvage was ordered wherever important collections of materials could be rescued, and the recovery of royal and official archives was given a high priority. On 29 November a detailed survey of the ruins was ordered to be made so that the extent of the properties destroyed would be on record to prevent future litigation about their exact sites and exact size. The engineers were made to control the disposal of debris, particularly the routes whereby it was to be shifted, a necessary precaution in the hilly city, and to arrange the siting of the rubble dumps and the levelling operations in the squares. Then, as soon as building could start again, limekilns for mortar and ovens for baking bricks and tiles had to be provided on a large scale, and in addition to the work on the public buildings about one thousand private houses were restored to a usable condition in the first year. It was, however, at once realized that Lisbon must be rebuilt according to a master plan, and from the very beginning of 1756 unauthorized building in stone or brick on sites in the ruined area was stopped. What this plan was and the nature of the economical Pombaline architecture can still be studied in the Terreiro do Paço and the grid of streets running out of it to the north (cf. Pl. V). As a result Lisbon provides today a classic example of eighteenth-century town-planning, influenced by Turin and by Covent Garden, and this famous rebuilding is Pombal's most magnificent achievement.

Pombal had, of course, to consider the situation outside Lisbon, and to provide relief for other towns that had suffered in the earthquake, in particular Setúbal, where the damage was bad. Another danger was that, taking advantage of the disorganization of the kingdom and a concentration of troops in the capital, the occasional raids of African pirates on the coast of Algarve, the southern littoral of Portugal, might develop into a serious ravaging of this vulnerable and earthquake-shaken district. Pombal therefore sent five companies of horse, to be based on Loulé and Faro and to patrol the danger-points, a measure that no doubt gave great comfort to the frightened inhabitants of this area.

The dislocation of trading and money transactions was soon one of the worst troubles in the emergency, and Pombal demanded that those engaged in essential occupations should continue to conduct their business, if it were possible to do so. This applied to all the useful trades, and to banking and exchange. The continuation of the printing-presses was also important, partly for the innumerable proclamations and orders that had to be posted over the city, and also to keep up a supply of general news about the world outside Portugal. The weekly *Gazeta de Lisboa* appeared on 5 November without its publication being interrupted, and the Spanish gazettes were soon on sale again. It was also necessary to restore the trade with the Portuguese colonies overseas, where the vastly exaggerated rumours about what had happened to Lisbon were causing merchants to suspend the dispatch of their ships with goods ready to export to Portugal; for this reason Portuguese warships, which could with great difficulty be spared, were sent to Brazil, India, and Africa to restore confidence. The first of these ships left for Pernambuco on 1 January 1756, and on its return did something to alleviate the shortage of sugar which was making the Portuguese particularly miserable.

The earthquake provided an opportunity for reducing the trading-privileges of the British; these depended on obligations imposed upon the Portuguese by treaty and were the jealously guarded rights of the Factory in Lisbon and of the British wine-merchants in Oporto. Pombal considered that these concessions were too generous. Immediately after the earthquake, the Junta de Commercio (Board of Trade), re-created by King José at Pombal's suggestion in September 1755, was briefed to protect Portuguese trade against English interests, if indeed that was not one of the principal reasons for its re-establishment, and the four per cent *Donativo*, the Junta's contribution to recovery of the city and costs of rebuilding the official and business quarters, was a direct tax on all imports into Lisbon of any origin, a tax that members of the British Factory considered to be in their case an illegal imposition. They claimed exemption, and were refused. In fact, they were far too eager in the period immediately following the earthquake to consolidate their former position as specially privileged merchants, and this gave Pombal an opportunity to snub them, which he did, as we must now admit fairly enough. The establishment in September 1756 of the Upper Douro Wine Company was another of Pombal's moves against the English privileges in Portugal, and, clumsy and inopportune though it proved to be, it further embittered relations between England and Portugal, in spite of traditional friendship many centuries old and the genuine and practical sympathy wholeheartedly offered to the Portuguese by the English at the time of the Lisbon earthquake.

At this point the outside opinion of Monsieur Ange Goudar, a young French writer on political economy, becomes sinisterly significant, though he overplayed his hand. He had been in Portugal in 1752 and had formed a very bad opinion of that country because of its foolish economic dependence on England, to whom in his view the Portuguese gold mines in Brazil now virtually belonged. The purpose of the little book he published in 1756 [10] was to explain to the Portuguese that even a disastrous earthquake could be turned into a positive blessing if it were made the occasion of a definite break with the rapacious country that had been meanly exploiting Portugal for so many years. He had already written a long book [11] on French economics, criticizing almost every

[10] *Relation historique du Tremblement de Terre . . . précédé d'un Discours politique.* A la Haye, 1756.
[11] *Les intérêts de la France mal entendus,* par un Citoyen. 3 vols. Amsterdam, 1756. Also a Paris production.

aspect of the political administration of his country, and in it he had commented sharply on the failure of the French to advance their business interests in Portugal. Now he explained why. England had conquered Portugal without the bother of a war, and a feeble, bankrupt Portuguese government accepted the situation. England now sold Portugal essential commodities at prices that made it not worth while for Portugal to produce them for themselves; for this reason Portuguese agriculture was ruined, and the Portuguese had to buy nearly all their cloth from England. They bought very little indeed from the equally good French market, and it paid the English to see that Portugal did not trade in a large way with anyone but themselves. England took the main output of the Brazilian gold mines, and England's prosperity was to a great extent dependent on this shameless scoop. The portrait of the Portuguese King, João V, on Brazilian gold coins, was better known in London than the portrait of King George II on English coins. If anything went wrong with the economic situation in England, a few bad harvests, for instance, Portugal would be completely ruined, and the earthquake should now bring this foolish sycophantic country to its senses. It was mentally backward; it was indifferent to science and the arts, and had become one of the most barbaric countries of Europe; but there was still a last chance.

To give point to his remarks Monsieur Goudar published with this *discours politique* a short account of the Lisbon earthquake and a summary of the heavy losses involved. He said the Inquisition was to blame for suppressing industry in Portugal and preventing the proper increase of knowledge, particularly scientific knowledge.

He said that what Portugal needed was not hordes of priests and monks, but many more labourers, craftsmen, business men, and soldiers. The Inquisition very naturally banned the book in a proclamation dated 8 October 1756, denouncing it as seditious, provocative, likely to disturb the peace and Portugal's foreign relations, and also offensive and abusive, insulting, contemptuous, and libellous in its references to Portugal. This was an inevitable verdict and sentence from the Church, but if the reckless young author kept Anglo-Portuguese relations under close observation during the next few years, he might have suspected that the Portuguese government, which was Pombal, had come very nearly to the same conclusions as himself.

In his directive of 3 November to the Patriarch about the quick disposal of the dead bodies, Pombal asked the Cardinal to do his best to stop the dreadful alarmist sermons that were terrifying the already nervous people of Lisbon by prophesying even greater disasters to come because of the enormity of the city's sins; for these passionately delivered discourses not only incited their hearers to panic and renewed attempts to escape from the neighbourhood of the city, but also suggested that the appropriate spiritual exercises should take precedence over the practical business of restoring order in Lisbon, and seemed to be reasons for resisting, as an irrelevant and wordly waste of time, the sensible endeavours of the government to provide for their bodily needs. This request by Pombal went straight to the heart of one of the most serious difficulties of the post-earthquake situation in Lisbon, as the next chapters will show. Pombal felt that what the people of Lisbon really needed was a strong, comforting assurance that the earthquake was not necessarily an angry God's chastisement of His sinful children, but, more probably, just an accidental natural occurrence. There does not seem to be any evidence that he desired to interfere with the Church's proper duties or the people's penitence and prayers; but he did not want the inhabitants of Lisbon frightened out of their plain duties to their neighbours and to the community of which they formed a part. For this reason good factual reporting of the disaster was an essential requirement, and it was also desirable that, however vehement the opposition might be, the scientists should be allowed to discuss their theories about the earthquake's cause.

Apart from the brief notices in the *Gazeta de Lisboa*, the first printed account of the earthquake in Portugal to attract attention was the *Carta* of José de Oliveira Trovão e Sousa, dated 20 December 1755 and published in Coimbra in that year.[12] It is a small pamphlet cast in the form of a letter to a friend who had asked particulars of the disaster from a writer who was in no mood for any belittling of the horrors he had witnessed. The earth, we are told, had opened in great yawning caverns; the seismic waves were so tremendous that the very sea-bed was exposed; the population gave way to violently emotional religious agonies expressed in tears, confessions, and acts of penitence; heretics became suddenly converted to the Roman faith. The loss of life was colossal, totalling about seventy thousand killed; practically the whole of Lisbon was uninhabitable. The damage elsewhere in Portugal

---

[12] *Carta em que hum amigo dá noticia a outro do lamentavel successo de Lisboa.* Coimbra, 1755.

was appalling. Setúbal was almost totally ruined and two thousand people were killed there; 120 died in Sintra; Santarém had lost most of its fine buildings. Only in Coimbra, where the author lived, was everything different. Coimbra suffered a violent shock, but the mighty arm of God was protecting the city, and the damage was negligible; Coimbra, conscience-stricken, at once devoted itself to the most elaborate religious exercises, so fervently and piously that Coimbra set an example to the whole of Portugal. Lisbon, on the other hand, one must sorrowfully infer, had received its deserts; for Lisbon was a very wicked city.

This preposterous account of the earthquake annoyed the sensible Portuguese, who understood how foolish it was to exaggerate a situation already very bad indeed. Protests were published quickly by two writers; the first a Franciscan, António dos Remédios, whose reply [13] is dated 20 January 1756, challenged the nonsense about the earth opening in great chasms and the sea-bed being exposed, and also the reckless statements about the numbers of the killed; the second, Bento Morganti (*see* p. 110), writing under the name José Acursio de Tavares in a pamphlet dated 13 February 1756,[14] said it was absurd to describe Lisbon as totally destroyed, since, except for a small part of the Alfama, and a considerable part of the districts of Rua Nova, Rossio, Remolares, and the Bairro Alto, Lisbon was still habitable.

The first sensible piece of reporting by a Portuguese author that was widely read is the *Commentary* by An-

[13] *Resposta a carta de José de Oliveira Trovão e Sousa.* Lisbon, 1756.
[14] *Verdade Vindicada, ou resposta a huma carta escrito de Coimbra.* Lisbon, 1756.

tónio Pereira (afterwards António Pereira de Figueiredo), a young priest of the Congregation of the Oratory who later became one of the most famous theologians of eighteenth-century Portugal (*see* p. 165). His account of the earthquake was published in Lisbon in 1756 in Latin and Portuguese,[15] and in London in Latin and English.[16] The Chevalier de Oliveira, a Portuguese exile in London who had become a Protestant, was greatly and unfairly offended by this publication (*see* p. 162), for it was coloured by a warmhearted Roman Catholic thought and spoke of miracles and the fate of sacred images, subjects that the author knew would be of great interest to the Roman communion all over the world. The little pamphlet began with the remark that the Lisbon earthquake was such a terrible event that one would think God had decided to punish the sins of many ages in a single day, and in a few vivid sentences António Pereira gave a gruesome picture of what had happened; but he said that there had been a number of amazing rescues of a miraculous nature, and on the practical side great credit must be given to the authorities for the care given to the wounded and the efficient disposal of the dead. Readers must be cautioned against exaggerated estimates of the numbers killed; in his own Oratory church where the Coimbra pamphlet said two hundred people had died, António Pereira had learnt from his brethren present at the time that at the most not more than fifty people had perished. He had made inquiries about casualties throughout all the religious orders, and he did not think more than

[15] *Commentario Latino e Portuguez sobre o terremoto e incendio de Lisboa. De que foy testemunha ocular seu Autor* . . . Lisbon, 1756.
[16] *A Narrative of the Earthquake and Fire of Lisbon by Anthony Pereira.* London, 1756.

two hundred professed members had lost their lives, and the total casualties of the earthquake he put at about fifteen thousand. He then gave a list of the buildings destroyed, correcting some of the statements in the Coimbra letter, and mentioning the rescue of the archives from the damaged Torre do Tombo; he then described the damage done by the fire, and lamented the disastrous loss of Lisbon's art collections and libraries; next, he spoke of the practical measures whereby a chaotically difficult situation had been quickly brought under control, and he said that the admirable work of the civil administration had been equalled by the inspiring direction of the Patriarch in religious matters.

That is a typical contemporary description of the Lisbon earthquake by an honest Portuguese writer, and there are several of its kind. On the other hand, the pamphlets suggesting that the Lisbon earthquake was a natural happening, like eclipses, thunder, rain, or anything else that was alarming or disastrous in man's celestial or terrestrial environment, are far fewer in number. To advocate this view openly was a bold act likely to shock most devout Portuguese people and anger their religious instructors, and it is at first only in short and rather carefully worded publications that this view, even though it had Pombal's full support, was advocated by Portuguese scientists resident in Portugal. One of the earliest to venture an opinion on this dangerous subject was the Marquesa de Tavora's doctor, José Alvares da Silva, whose work is dated from the Campo Pequeno [17] on 6 December 1755.[18] The

[17] The Palácio Galveias, now the Biblioteca Municipal Central, in the Campo Pequeno, was a Tavora residence.
[18] *Investigação das causas proximas do Terremoto, succedido em Lisboa no anno de 17$\frac{11}{1}$55. Por J. A. da S. Lisbon, 1756.

earthquake, he said, might be a judgement of God upon the Portuguese; but da Silva insisted that earthquakes could also be naturally caused, and he explained that there were several scientific theories suggesting how and why they happened; compressed air, for instance, is a likely explanation, and electricity may be an important factor. It is true enough that God must be ultimately the cause of every earthquake, but that is not a sufficient reason for supposing that the Lisbon earthquake was a result of Lisbon's wickedness. It is ridiculous to compare Lisbon with Babylon, and if God intended by this example to show His anger against atheists and free-thinkers, there were obviously other countries far more deserving of His divine chastisement. The real point is that it is a duty to find out how nature works, before we decide that what may be natural events are supernatural; we must study experimental physics seriously and learn what natural forces can perform. The world would be spiritually poorer without the results of the researches of men like Descartes or Newton, and it was, said da Silva, a very fortunate thing for Portugal that some of the Portuguese nobility, particularly the fourth Conde da Ericeira (1673-1743), had realized that the physical sciences must be encouraged.

Another author who stood shoulder to shoulder with da Silva was Miguel Tibério Pedegache Brandão Ivo, a young military man of Swiss descent who was a native of Lisbon and was well-read in science. He gave, first of all, a purely factual description of the disaster and a long dissertation about subterranean fires, but his final suggestion was that the moon may have something to do with the cause of an earthquake, as also the heat of the sun.[19] Yet another writer who was concerned exclusively with scientific causes, and even dared to rebuke the alarmist preachers, was Veríssimo António Moreira de Mendonça, a great advocate of the central fire theory and brother of Joachim José de Mendonça, whose longer study of earthquakes and description of the Lisbon one, published in 1758, with an alternative scientific explanation, will be presently mentioned. Immediately, however, we come to a book of far greater significance than any of the brief scientific papers of which we have been speaking, a medical treatise by a celebrated Portuguese doctor of European fame who was living in France, António Nunes Ribeiro Sanches (1699-1783).

The Portuguese had not neglected the medical aspects of the earthquake. They dreaded the outbreak of a plague, a calamity well known to Lisbon, and their frantic concern about getting rid of the corpses and restoring some sort of drainage system was a sensible expression of this fear. The medical men available in Lisbon were no doubt far too few in numbers and were not properly trained to deal with this emergency; but they did their best and understood the danger that threatened the city. The Tavora house-doctor, José Alvares da Silva, whose scientific *Investigação* has been already mentioned, wrote another pamphlet,[20] dated 16 March 1756, in which he showed that the risk of infection from the putrefaction of the corpses was not as serious as might be thought. He said there was good reason for supposing, as Dr. Mead in

[19] *Nova e Fiel Relação do Terremoto que experimentou Lisboa e todo Portugal no 1 de Novembro 1755, com algumas observacions curiosas e a explicação das suas causas.* Por M. T. P. Lisbon, 1756.

[20] *Precauções Medicas contra algumas remotas consequencias, que se podem excitar do Terremoto de 17$\frac{1}{1}$55.* Lisbon, 1756.

England had suggested, that plagues start in Africa and nowhere else, and even if conditions in Lisbon were obviously disquieting, at least it should be remembered that the dreadful consuming fire had compensating purgative properties, having performed wholesale sanitary cremations, and also that a mercifully persistent north wind had cleared the city seawards of all noxious odours; moreover, as it was winter, some corpses had been protected from doing harm by partial refrigeration, and others had been to some appreciable extent mummified by copious deposits of tar and ashes. On the other hand, though plague does not come from rotting bodies, a large number of lesser ailments may do so, and it is extremely important to observe certain fundamental rules of hygiene, particularly those that keep the blood pure; da Silva then explained what sensible people ought to do in the matter of diet and exercise and the use of disinfectants and frequent changes into clean clothes. He stressed the value of mental confidence and refusal to panic, and he suggested that music was very important as a sedative; he then prescribed various medicines to cure the preliminary disorders that might seem to be the beginning of a much more serious illness. Finally, he paid a most respectful tribute to his great friend Ribeiro Sanches, who had written to express his approval of what da Silva said, and that is a deserved introduction to the book that was shortly to arrive in Lisbon written by this famous man, one of the foremost physicians in Europe.

António Nunes Ribeiro Sanches (1699-1783), who was of Jewish origin, had taken his degree in Coimbra, had worked in a plague in Lisbon in 1723, and had afterwards studied in Geneva, London, Paris, and with Boerhaave in Leiden, and had been an honoured physician in the Russian imperial court. His contribution to his country's needs in the hour of its agony was the publication in 1756 in Paris of a long book [21] on the maintenance of the public health. It was anonymous and had a dedication to the Duque de Lafões by Pedro Gendron,[22] but it was on sale in Lisbon as well as in Paris, and there does not seem to have been any mystery about the identity of its author. The book is said to have had the warm approval of Pombal, as is indeed likely, for the manual was plainly intended to be of practical use to the authorities responsible for the recovery of Lisbon, and it was indeed the best possible antidote to an unsettling religious hysteria. Ribeiro Sanches said that the medical control of a community depended on the observation of certain simple rules and regulations safeguarding the health of the people, and he thought that every responsible person ought to know what these rules are and the principles underlying them; he had specially in mind heads of religious institutions, hospitals and prisons, military and naval commanders, and fathers of families. Ribeiro Sanches was particularly anxious that architects should also study the handbook, so that new buildings should be sanitary and well-aired, and he also emphasized how important it was for the Portuguese to study the health of their sailors, for the capital was exposed to risk of diseases brought by ships from their world-wide dominions. Fresh

[21] *Tratado da conservação da Saude dos Povos: obra util, e igualmente necessaria a os Magistrados, Capitaens Generais, Capitaens de Mar e Guerra, Prelados, Abbadessas, Medicos, e Pays de Familia: com hum Appendix. Consideracions sobre os Terremotos* . . . Paris, e se vende em Lisboa, 1756.

[22] A Parisian bookseller, later known as an editor of Camões.

air and cleanliness were his main requirements, and he had a great deal to say about ventilation and sanitary regulations, diseases common in barracks, camps, and ships, and suitable dietary treatment. Finally, Ribeiro Sanches said that medical schools in Portugal needed encouragement and improvement, and he urged that young medical men should not be allowed to practice without adequate previous experience of clinical work. Then came an appendix about earthquakes and their causes. He reviewed the principal ancient and modern scientific theories in order to make it quite clear that all who have considered the matter carefully treat earthquakes as natural events, for which reason ignorant, timid, superstitious people should be strongly discouraged from regarding them in terror as supernatural events. Their attitude spreads alarm and a sense of hopelessness. We are not afraid any more in that way of thunder or lightning; we do not regard violent tempests as terrifying prodigies with moral implications; we have got used to horrors like war, which man makes every bit as destructive as anything nature can do; we accept gunpowder, fire, and poison as ordinary hazards of life, and we do not believe these things strike at us under supernatural instruction as a punishment for our sins. Only when earthquakes are concerned do we slip back into our panicky primitive fears. We must now try to get used to thinking of earthquakes as we think of storms, and to realize that they are really very common occurrences. God *may* use an earthquake to punish mankind. That must be admitted. But the majority of earthquakes cannot possibly have a moral significance, and we are very foolish to worry about them on the grounds that they are punishments and warnings of further impending disasters.

It was in Spain and not in Portugal that the controversy about the cause of earthquakes had its oddest airing in print. It began when an ingenious scientist, Juan Luis Roche of Puerto de Santa Maria in the Gulf of Cádiz, published an account of the effects of the earthquake of 1 November in that little town. This is in the form of a letter, dated 12 November, to the various learned academies with which he was connected, and in these he gave a very careful description of the shock and the subsequent seismic wave.[23] He studied the positions of the fallen masonry, using a compass, and had theories about the direction in which the earthquake had moved, and he measured as far as possible the extent of the flooding that did so much damage in the lower part of the town. He said he had no new explanation to offer of the cause of earthquakes, as much had already been written on the various scientific explanations of them; but he did not think any of them was entirely satisfactory. He was concerned simply with a record of what happened, and as this is unfolded we find that while Dr. Roche was a good scientist writing for fellow-scientists, he was also in reasonable agreement with much that the more superstitious clergy were saying about the earthquake. His view seems to have been that though science can explain how an earthquake happens, nevertheless when one does take

[23] *Relación y Observaciones physicas-mathematicas, y morales sobre el general Terremoto y la Irrupción del Mar . . . que comprendió a la Ciudad y Gran Puerto de Santa Maria, y a toda la Costa, y Tierra firme del reyno de Andalucia. Es una Carta que escrivio D.J.L.R.* Puerto de Santa Maria, 1755.

place it is in spite of its natural causes supernaturally controlled. He had no difficulty in accepting a variety of miracles that took place in Puerto de Santa Maria in connexion with the events of 1 November, and he believed, for example, that the seismic wave was checked and repulsed by the Virgin Mary. In fact, Roche held that an earthquake could not be dismissed as a purely natural event, for one could actually observe what could only be the providential control of the shock's effects. Take Seville, for instance. Why did the Giralda remain standing after the earthquake on 1 November? It is 350 feet high with a heavy belfry and bronze finial at the top; its walls have to take a strain in an earthquake ten times greater than a thirty-foot tower, and oscillate over an arc ten times greater. Yet, whereas many smaller towers did collapse in this earthquake, the Giralda was not destroyed. Why? Because God had protected it.

The next event, which seems to have startled Spain almost as much as the earthquake itself, was the publication by Roche of a pronouncement on the cause of earthquakes by the most respected and most outspoken of all the learned men in Spain, the famous Benito Jerónimo Feyzóo y Montenegro (1676-1764), a Benedictine living in Oviedo and then eighty years old. Feyzóo referred to Roche as his intimate and ingenious friend, and that was a great honour for the Andalusian, as the prestige of the celebrated old man was by this time enormous. He was renowned for his fearless denunciation of medieval habits of thought, dubious miracles—he had written a poem denouncing an alleged miracle in Roche's Puerto de Santa Maria, pointing out that it was just due to reflection [24]

[24] Feyzóo: *Adiciones á las Obras*, p. 17. Madrid, 1783.

—the superstitious teaching of the clergy, obsolete educational methods, the cold-shouldering of modern scientific knowledge, and almost everything that was unprogressive and backward in Spain; but because of his piety he had escaped any severe official condemnation and because of his skill and sincerity in confounding those who were imprudent enough to challenge him, his influence was very great indeed and his lightest word listened to with a genuine respect. As we see it now, Feyzóo was not an important scientist, and his remarks on the cause of earthquakes are nothing more than some modest and casual speculations of a learned old man put forward in the course of writing a few letters on a subject that much interested him; but Roche regarded these letters as a literary and scientific scoop that would cause a sensation in Spain, and he published them in Puerto de Santa Maria in 1756 with the impressive title, *A New Theory about the physical cause of Earthquakes, now explained by electric phenomena, and specially adapted to the shock felt in Spain on November 1st 1755.*[25] This arresting work is packed out with a variety of prefaces and preliminary essays by Roche himself and some young scientific friends in Seville.

The letters were written by Feyzóo in Oviedo in December 1755 and January 1756, and the first four were addressed to Josef Díaz de Guitian of Cádiz, and the fifth to a canon of Toledo Cathedral who had asked Fey-

---

[25] *Nuevo Systhema sobre la causa physica de los Terremotos, explicado por los phenomenos electricos, y adaptado al que padeció España en 1° de Noviembre del año antecedente de 1755.* Su autor El Illmo. y Rmo. Senor Don Fray Benito Geronymo Feyzóo, Ex-General de la Religion de San Benito, del Conseio de su Majestad, etc. Puerto de Santa Maria, 1756.

zóo to say something that would lessen the general alarm caused throughout Spain by the earthquake of 1 November. In the first letter Feyzóo wondered if the frequent earthquakes of the eighteenth century could be due to a gradual contraction of the earth's substance, a crumbling and cracking-up of the globe that was bound to end up in a portentous calamity; but he went on to say that if the earthquake in the Iberian peninsula on 1 November had been felt also in France, foreign scientists would have had quite a good case for attributing the cause to the newly fashionable cause of everything, namely electricity. In his third letter he returns again to the strange fact that earthquakes happen simultaneously at points far distant one from another, and by this time he had collected a considerable amount of information on the subject. In the case of the last earthquake both Cádiz and Oviedo experienced the shock at precisely the same time, 9:45 A.M., a matter on which Feyzóo could speak with some certainty as in Oviedo the Cathedral clock and the Benedictine College clock were excellent timekeepers. Yet Oviedo and Cádiz were nearly five hundred miles apart. Interior conflagrations and explosions cannot possibly explain this, so that the electricity theory had to be taken seriously, and he said he was now prepared to support the idea, on the supposition that *materia electrica,* though deeply embedded in the earth, could reach instantly to the earth's upper caverns, however far apart they might be situated and explode at the same moment the combustible gasses that had been collecting in them.[26]

26 This was not a new suggestion, for William Stukeley in England (see p. 18) and Andrea Bina in Italy, *Ragionamente sopra la cagione de' Tremuoti,* first published in 1751 and republished in 1756, had proposed similar theories.

In the fifth letter Feyzóo left this gentle scientific speculation in order to explain that the popular fear of earthquakes was rather ridiculous. There was no reason to
dread earthquakes in the way that people do. There is
a much greater risk of sudden death from other causes,
and this should be realized and we should all of us so
order our lives that we are prepared for sudden death.
As a grim warning to the heedless, Feyzóo mentioned the
dreadful end of an adulterous couple who were found
dead in each other's arms in an inn in Galicia.

Juan Luis Roche was impressed and also a little jealous
when he read these letters. Electricity was *his* subject, and
he believed he was the first person to experiment with
an electrical machine in Spain. He had said in his *Relación* that he was doubtful about the current scientific explanations of earthquakes, and he now felt it should have
been understood that he was already considering whether
electricity might not be their real cause. Some of his scientific friends were inclined to take his side, and his publication of the *Nuevo Systhema* is not only a tribute to
Feyzóo, whom he did sincerely admire, but also a fairly
plain hint that Seville had very little to learn from Oviedo.
In fact, scientific Seville had something very important to
say, not particularly about Feyzóo and the electricity
theory, but about a proper attitude towards earthquakes.

Roche called to his aid two young scientists in Seville,
and all three no doubt considered that under the shelter
of Feyzóo's letters science could now state its case with
great confidence and show how absurd it was for the
people to be terrified by the common talk that God
caused earthquakes in order to punish those who had offended Him. The first of the two young men who con-

tributed essays to the *Nuevo Systhema* was José Cevallos
(1726-76) of Seville University, a man with a brilliant
career ahead of him as theologian, scientist, academician,
and Rector of the University. He was full of praise for
Feyzóo, and sure that it was right to do everything possible to discover the scientific cause of earthquakes, for,
after all, common safety depended on the possession of
much more accurate information about their cause and
effects; but he did not feel at all sure that Feyzóo had
solved the problem. He objected to the theory that Seville and Lisbon were connected by an earthquake-track,
as historical records did not support the view that these
two cities generally suffered earthquakes simultaneously,
and he did not by any means trust the electricity theory.
He did not think people really knew much about it yet.
Feyzóo was impressed by Musschenbroek's painful experiment with the Leiden jar in which he had nearly electro-
cuted himself; [27] but Cevallos had tried it for himself, and
he had got no result worse than a shock in the arm, the
effect of which lasted for a fortnight. Cevallos then went
on to say how much he liked Feyzóo's fifth letter, and he
turned rather abruptly on the Seville clergy; they should
show themselves much more ready to give absolution in
cases of accidents and emergencies; their record on the
day of the earthquake was very bad. Here the young man
makes his main point. Earthquakes are part of the ordinary hazards of life, like accidents in the street. God

[27] Feyzóo probably got his information about the jar experiment from
the Abbé Mangins, *Histoire générale et particulière de l'Electricité,* Paris,
1752 (published anonymously). He had also the *Mémoires of the Aca-
demie des Sciences* (année 1746, p. 2) and the Abbé J. A. Nollet's works
on electricity, one of which had been translated into Spanish by J. Vaz-
quez y Morales, *Ensayo sobre la Electricidad de los Cuerpos,* prefaced
by a brief *Historia de la Electricidad.* Madrid, 1747.

may be their ultimate cause, but that does not mean that the earthquake-dead have been supernaturally executed on special divine instruction. Ignorant preaching on the supernatural origin had done great harm, and theologians who would not acquaint themselves with modern thought are much to be blamed.

The second essay on Feyzóo's letters in this extraordinary publication was written by Francisco de Buendia y Ponce (1721-1800), a young medical man in holy orders who, like Cevallos, afterwards became a famous scholar and writer. He wanted to express his view of a doctor's responsibility in the matter of confession and absolution; [28] for he was deeply concerned about the hazards of sudden death, and he capped the Oviedo story of the adulterous couple with a tale of two couples of young Andalusian adulterers who got imprisoned in a cave on the shore of the Guadalquivir into which they entered in order to indulge their wicked passions; a fall of rock shut them in, and they were not found until a week or so later when dogs scented their rotting bodies.

Then Juan Luis Roche himself introduced the master's letters in a long preface. He was now writing as a courageous scientist, full of praise for his pet electricity and its formidable powers; he felt it his duty to denounce the popular attitude to earthquakes, which took the form of a mood of hysterical and superstitious religious fear followed quickly by forgetfulness and flippancy. Today's tears are quickly replaced by tomorrow's dances, and lamentations give way to insolent jesting on sacred subjects. In Seville, at the time when he wrote, one could find fans, ribbons, shoes, songs, and dances, all with frivolous earth-

[28] Cf. Feyzóo on this subject, *Cartas Eruditas,* v, Carta XII.

quake-allusions, and that sort of thing, said Roche, is an insult to the proper fear of God.

Feyzóo's pronouncement, published under these wordy and enthusiastic auspices, made a very great impression, and argument about his views continued into 1757. Dr. Miguel Cabrera of Seville and the aged Bishop of Guadix, Miguel de San José, refuted this new electricity theory, and the Bishop spoke somewhat sharply about the reluctance of Dr. Cevallos to recognize the operation of the divine hand in an earthquake. He was quite prepared to meet the scientists on their own ground. Science was no mystery; it was a subject taught at the theological colleges, and the clergy were quite capable of exposing fallacies such as those evident in Feyzóo's electricity theory and in the presumption of Copernicus, who had tried to halt the sun and move the earth. They had, however, the additional advantage of being trained in a superior science, *pneumatologia,* the science of spirits. Frankly, the Bishop believed that earthquakes were caused by evil spirits who had obtained, God permitting it, a temporary malevolent control of those forces of nature that people like Dr. Cevallos now supposed to be the exclusive province of scientific speculation.

Feyzóo had indeed alarmed conservative Hispanic thought. From Toledo the Licenciado Juan de Zuñiga protested to the great man himself; he said that earthquakes were God's most frightful way of showing His anger and that man's sins were undoubtedly their real cause. Feyzóo replied kindly that it was a pious duty to bear such considerations in mind. This was not considered a very satisfactory answer, and Portugal intervened in the person of a young lawyer, Feliciano da Cunha França, who wrote a disapproving pamphlet of fifty pages on the misplaced interest of Feyzóo and others in the scientific causes of the earthquake. He knew for certain that what had happened in Lisbon had been directly ordered by God in order to punish sin.

In Seville Dr. José Cevallos decided to answer Miguel de San José, the Bishop of Guadix. He said he was not prepared to defend the electricity theory. Electricity was a new-fangled thing, made by a machine, not mentioned in the Bible, and there is really no evidence that in antiquity, or at any time in Spain, there was such a force. He agreed wholeheartedly that God is rightly regarded as the original cause of all earthquakes; but God may have many motives in permitting earthquakes to take place, and of ten possible reasons anger against sinners is the last. All the evidence suggests that the great earthquake of 1 November 1755 was a natural earthquake. It was, of course, right to fear earthquakes, to pray God to deliver men from them, and to try to improve one's conduct as a result of them. He cited with admiration Bishop Gaspar de Villaroel of Santiago, Chile, who had experienced the great earthquake there in May 1647; this prelate had been so disgusted by the lies, false miracles, revelations, prophecies, and so on, that had followed the disaster, such as had disgusted Cevallos in Seville, that he boldly declared before all the world that he saw no reason to suppose that earthquakes were always punishments for the sins of the people who lived in the towns destroyed by their agency.[29] Cevallos said the clergy had a heavy duty laid upon them at the time of an earth-

---

[29] Gaspar de Villaroel: *Govierno Ecclesiastico Pacifico,* ii, p. 581. Madrid, 1738.

quake. They should instruct the public on behaviour, confession, prayer, and divine providence, and they should
discredit, instead of spreading, silly stories about devils
lurking over the city, and about worse destruction to
come, and also about the miraculous behaviour of images.
Lies such as that there had never been an earthquake in
Rome, or in Toledo, the second Rome, could be and
should be disproved. The really important thing, said
Cevallos, was to make it generally known that the public welfare required a scientific investigation of the causes
and behaviour of earthquakes in order that there should
be in the future warnings before they happened, houses
built to withstand their shock, an escape-drill, and train-
ing in fire-fighting.

Some of the Portuguese were of the same opinion, and
the best example of this kind of sensible study of the
Lisbon earthquake was published in 1758. It was the work
of Joachim José Moreira de Mendonça, an official of the
Torre do Tombo archive in the Castle, who was in the
Castle precincts when the earthquake happened. His account is a document of great value for it was compiled
with a controlling regard for accuracy, and it was Moreira
de Mendonça who first corrected the story of the total
engulfing of the Cais de Pedra, João V's fine new marble
quay in the Terreiro do Paço, a story still repeated as
one of the most frightful occurrences on the earthquake
day. The main interest of his book, however, is that it
is designed on a grand scale and has the imposing title
História Universal dos Terremotos; for he thought that a
full history of all the recorded earthquakes of the past
would show them to be common events and so diminish

the horrors of the disaster that had lately befallen Lisbon. At the same time he believed that a demonstration of the frequency of earthquakes would warn his readers of an ever-present danger, so that, firstly, they should do their best to lead good lives and keep their consciences clear, in order that, whatever happened, their souls would not perish, and, secondly, so that they should learn to build stronger houses in the reasonable hope that they need not even lose their lives. Moreira de Mendonça's concern for souls was prudent as it made it possible for the Inquisition censor to decide that he was a good *philosophe* and a good historian who could write about the natural causes of earthquakes without forgetting the moral lessons they are meant to enforce, and without in any way offending against the teaching of his most holy faith.

Moreira de Mendonça, who said he was an extremely busy man with little time to spare for writing, was obviously well-read in science before the earthquake and a thoughtful man well-qualified for the task he set himself. When he came to his dissertation on geo-physics, Moreira de Mendonça said that though we could not possibly hope to comprehend all the mysteries of the universe, God did make the world we live in for us men, and it is presumably His wish that we should try to find out all we can about its nature. Men have dwelt on the earth for a long time, and still the world is full of apparently unfathomable secrets, and many would say that earthquakes are among the inexplicable phenomena; but on another view they are a challenge to our intelligence that we must accept. Admittedly, it is difficult to investigate their causes by direct observation and testing, but it is nevertheless our duty to think out an explanation that is based on what little we do know about geology and mechanics and is also in agreement with the observable laws of nature.

After a short summary of the older explanations of earthquakes, Moreira de Mendonça turns suddenly to an exposure of what he considered to be the feeble and misleading views on this subject of his contemporaries in Portugal. He is made angry by any theory based on the sole agency of a perpetual fire raging in the bowels of the earth, and nothing really pleased him in the Portuguese pamphlets on the science of earthquake causes; even his own brother, since dead, was in his view on the wrong track. The Spanish literature he liked better, and he singled out for praise the *Disertación física* of Dr. Francisco Martínez Moles of the University of Alcalá, who, though he did believe in the subterranean fire, nevertheless thought that earthquakes were caused by its effect on air and water under the earth. Moreira de Mendonça rightly understood that the grand old man Feyzóo was not putting forward his electricity theory in a serious way; he was just speculating about possible causes, and both Father Miguel Cabrera of Seville and the learned Bishop of Guadix had convincingly demolished his case; nevertheless, electricity was a new subject, and very interesting, so that Feyzóo *Nuevo Systhema* should be mentioned, if only to introduce to Portugal the opinions of such distinguished people as Feyzóo and Juan Luis Roche. After all this, Moreira de Mendonça gives us his own view about the actual causes of an earthquake,[30] which is that

[30] The contemporary earthquake-theories of Hispanic writers mentioned by Moreira de Mendonça are: (1) Portugal. João António da Costa, *Con-*

suggested by the Spanish writer, Moles, namely the explosive force of imprisoned air and water when heated by fire inside the earth. According to Moreira de Mendonça air and water circulate everywhere in the interior caverns of the earth, and in the earth there is an enormous amount of latent fire in the form of inflammable elements intermixed in all the materals of which earth, air, and water are made. All these materials are penetrable by, and kept in a state of movement by, ether, and they are continually acting upon each other. Fire therefore may originate accidentally at any time inside the earth either by spontaneous combustion or by fermentation, and it is these sudden conflagrations, however caused, that turn air and water in contact with them into the enormously powerful explosive force that is capable of causing an earthquake.

Some writers who explained what they believed to be the physical causes of the earthquake were also anxious to acknowledge that such a dreadful event might also be interpreted as God's moral judgement on a sinful city. There is, for instance, an account of the disaster, dated 16 December 1755, by Bento Morganti (b. 1709), a Lisbon priest of half-Italian parentage with numismatic, ar-

---

versação Erudita (*see* p. 111); J. Alvares da Silva, *Investigação* (*see* p. 92); José Xavier de Valadares e Sousa, *Terraemotus . . . Poetica Descriptio,* whose unscriptural view that the earth was once a planetary ball of fire is particularly to be condemned; Veríssimo António de Moreira de Mendonça (d. 1756), *Dissertação Philosophica sobre o Terremoto de Portugal,* the author's brother, another mistaken advocate of the central fire theory; and Feliciano da Cunha França, *Extenção de Dictamen . . . do . . . Feyzóo* (*see* p. 105), who is severely handled as he was imprudent enough to criticize the accuracy of Veríssimo António. (2) Spain. In addition to Moles, Feyzóo, Cabrera, and the Bishop of Guadix, Moreira de Mendonça refers to a *carta* of António Jacobo del Barco y Gasco, published in *Discursos Mercuriales XIV;* Juan de Zuñiga (*see* p. 105) and Francisco Mariano Nifo y Cagigal, *Explicación physico y moral de las causas . . . de los terremotos.* Madrid, 1755.

chaeological, and scientific interests, in which the author had much to say about the miracles that happened during the earthquake, particularly those connected with the images of Our Lady (cf. p. 119), and the reasonableness of imploring God to restrain the natural forces whereby He chastised His sinful children; yet, Bento Morganti said, really and truly earthquakes are nothing but natural phenomena caused by the violent explosions of mixed fire and air in the bowels of the earth.[31] Similarly, João António da Costa e Andrade, a lawyer of Santarém, in an elaborate discussion [32] about the effects of the earthquake in his native town and its neighbourhood, introduces a philosopher to explain the actual causes of the earthquake and a priest to argue strongly that the earthquake was primarily a supernatural portent. In the same way the learned Nifo of Madrid said in the introduction to his excusively scientifical study [33] of earthquakes that so far as the last one was concerned, shockingly bad behaviour in church and some quite unmentionable sins explained satisfactorily in his view why God had allowed the disaster of 1 November 1755 to happen.

Joachim José and Veríssimo António Moreira de Mendonça, on the other hand, did not agree about what was happening in the interior of the earth, but they were united in their contempt of the notion that the Lisbon earthquake was the consequence of Lisbon's sins. They did not even entertain the idea. Veríssimo António in the

[31] *Carta de hum amigo para outro em que se dá succinta noticia dos effeitos de Terremoto . . . com alguns principios fisicos para se conhecer a origem e causa natural de similhantes phenoménos terrestres.* Lisbon, 1756.

[32] *Conversação Erudita, Discurso Familiar, Conferencias Asceticas, Historicas, Politicas e Philosophicas.* Lisbon, 1756.

[33] See footnote, pp. 109-10.

preface to his little pamphlet said it was praiseworthy that other writers should refer to the moral causes of the earthquake, but he personally had no intention or inclination to preach a sermon on this subject. No sermon could be more effective than the immediate fear of God that the earthquake itself occasioned. He and other scientists (though here not his brother) believed that it was Hell fire, or something very like it, that caused the earthquake, and therefore there was quite enough for everybody to be frightened about without any pious persuasion. Joachim José thought that even this mild concession to the current theological ravings was rather silly. He explained to the best of his ability the physical causes of an earthquake. All he had to say after that was—let us adore the omnipotence of the Creator who causes all these secret happenings of nature, and let us recognize the incompetence of our finite understanding in the presence of the inscrutable operations of an infinite Being. Joachim José Moreira de Mendonça had nothing to say about Lisbon's abominable sins; nothing to say about the wrath of God.

Chapter Four

THE WRATH OF GOD (1)

The first effect of so shattering a disaster on the minds of most of the ordinary people is a complete surrender to the feeling that men and women are powerless puppets in a for ever broken world. It seems that there is nothing to be done but to run away from the blazing ruins and lament, aimlessly and hopelessly, a calamity beyond human comprehension and beyond human remedy. This mood changed quickly in Lisbon under the immediate comfort of Pombal's firm handling and bustling orders; but directly opposed to his steadying influence and to the straight-forward task of reorganization and repair was the bitter religious despondency caused by the common belief that the origin of the great earthquake was supernatural. If this were a deliberate chastisement by God of a sinful people, as was generally asserted by the clergy, the mechanical task of recovery was of little importance compared with a first and pressing duty of making peace with God and imploring Him not to punish further His now penitent people. It is understandable that in a deeply religious land this should quickly become a dominant thought, and to sustain it there came from all sides abundant evidence of miraculous happenings that attested the supernatural character of the earthquake; moreover, it was not long before elaborate public acts of contrition gave open expression to this feeling and acknowledged the wickedness of a population thus humbled beneath the scourge of a still wrathful God.

An indication of the public attitude was the appointment of St. Francis Borgia, who had died in 1572, as special patron and protector of the realm against further earthquakes and similar disasters, it being already known that the Jesuit saint was proficient to a high degree in warding off such horrors.[1] At the special request of the King, submitted through Pombal, the Pope, Benedict XIV, made the appointment in May 1756, and people felt much comforted thereby. St. Francis, fourth Duke of Gandía, on the east coast of Spain, and third General of the Jesuits, great-grandson of the Borgia Pope, Alexander VI, had had a Portuguese wife, Leonor de Castro, and during his lifetime he had on occasion been closely connected with Portuguese affairs. Now, the King of Portugal claimed relationship with him, and in Coimbra, where there was the earliest Jesuit college in Portugal and where the university was believed to be the object of his special care, the new patron was welcomed with elaborate religious celebrations and described as a saint who was "in large measure" Portuguese. With St. Francis as protector, it was felt that nothing could go wrong, and, though Lisbon continued to suffer alarmingly from repeated earthquakes over many months, in Coimbra at

---

[1] Even so, he did not get the post without competition from St. Theotonius and the Martyrs of Morocco; St. Agatha, enormously successful in dealing with Sicilian earthquakes and eruptions of Etna, was also recommended; see *Vida Prodigiosa da grande Virgen, e Martyr Sta Agueda especialissima Advogada contra os Incendios, e Terremotos.* Lisbon, 1756.

any rate nothing much did happen in the way of further shocks.

There were many stories of miraculous happenings during and after the earthquake, of wonderful healing without the aid of doctors or medicines, and particularly of escapes from death so marvellous that it could only be supposed in these cases Heaven had arrested the laws of nature. People emerged unharmed from painful imprisonment in the ruins that lasted several days; one little girl of fifteen who had been trapped clutching an image of St. Anthony was found safe and unhurt by Cardinal Sampaio of the Patriarchal Church in the wreckage of her home in the Rua dos Canos behind São Domingos after nine days without food. The bodies of officiating priests who had been killed were sometimes found in a state of miraculous preservation. In the Hermitage of Nossa Senhora da Vitoria in the parish of São Nicolau in the lower town the vested body of a Carmelite priest who had been celebrating Mass was found completely uncrushed or damaged after three or four months of burial under the rubble, though there was a charred, corrupted body close beside him.

One very important and consoling discovery was that the catastrophe of 1 November was not a cruelly sudden stroke that fell without warning; however wicked they might have been, the people thought God should have given them some advance notice of the punishment to come in order that there might be an opportunity for repenting; and, in fact, it was found that Lisbon had been told of the coming disaster by prophecies to which insufficient attention had been paid. Christ Himself had told Maria Joanna, a nun living in Louriçal, that He was deeply offended by the wickedness of Portugal, particularly the sins of Lisbon, and that appropriate punishment was shortly to be inflicted on this graceless people. The saintly lady died in March 1755, but the warning of her vision had become well known by 1754. It was now realized that her prayers alone had caused the expected punishment to be delayed until after her death; but by that time the accumulation of sins, added to the blatant disregard of her message, made the chastisement, when it did come, the more severe. Another nun had five times told her confessor of the impending disaster, imploring him to bid the people mend their ways and pray to be spared from their awful fate; but her message was ignored. The most desperate efforts were made to turn the unforeseen into the foreseen. In 1752 a Sebastianist, that is to say a believer in the messianic return of King Sebastian, whose death at the battle of Alcazar-Kebir in 1578 was the prelude to the Castilian usurpation, had prophesied that on All Saints' Day a formidable event would herald the arrival of the messiah at Cacilhas and Lisbon on two stated dates in the following spring. Nothing happened on All Saints' Day in 1752, and the prophecy was circulated again for 1753, and then, after a second failure, for 1754. When an earthquake did happen on All Saints' Day, 1755, the prophecy was recalled without its Sebastianist context or memory of its previous failures, and the people said Portugal had had a wonderful prophet who had foretold the earthquake.

There were also prophecies, after the event, of even worse misfortune to follow that would complete the punishment of Lisbon, prophecies to which the continuing series of earth-tremors gave a most unpleasant significance. It was rumoured that as on the first day of November so on the last day of that month there would be another colossal quake. As this did not take place, the second earthquake was promised for the fortieth day after the first, and then for other dates in December and January. On the night of 30 April 1756 timorous people stayed awake all night in gardens and open spaces, dreading an awful earthquake that a priest had said would take place on 1 May. He was imprisoned, but the foolish prophecies continued. The approach of 1 November 1756, the first anniversary of the great earthquake, was likewise dreaded as an obvious occasion on which Lisbon was going to be finally obliterated. A nun of Semide, close to Coimbra, is named as one of the culprits whose prophecies spread alarm at this time, and the Jesuits, rightly or wrongly, were also blamed. By 29 October the scare had become so great that a proclamation had to be issued forbidding anyone to leave Lisbon under any pretext during the next three days, and the city was ringed with troops. A light shock on the night of the twenty-ninth naturally made matters worse. This deliberate agitation of nerves already seriously upset seems to have been a persistent nuisance, and it was done sometimes quite deliberately by robbers who wanted to pillage the premises they had frightened people into evacuating; but there was also a steady supply of religious eccentrics telling the people that there was going to be an even bigger earthquake, or a colossal flood, or a total burning-up of the land by the sun. The worst offender was known as the Prophet of Leiria, but one sensible Franciscan who was protesting against these harmful prognostications also blamed "letters from Rome" and the activities of priests in Lisbon. Another wise writer traced the Sebastianist prophecy back to its source; but the scared inhabitants of Lisbon paid no attention. Most of them were in a mood to believe anything.[2]

To all this was added in the first days after the earthquake distress at many reported cases of the destruction of the consecrated Host and of sacred images in the churches and in the homes of the people. There were some brave and successful escapes from ruined and burning churches by priests who, abandoning all other duties, risked their lives in order to get the Host to a place of safety; but rescue was not always possible, and an agonizing consciousness of brutal sacrilege committed made the horrors of the earthquake worse.

The fate of the images caused equal pain, for all were loved, and many were famous objects of veneration believed to be endowed with miraculous powers. At least twenty figures of Christ could work miracles, and two or three of them could speak; there were over a dozen celebrated images of the Virgin with notable miraculous powers; and some of the hundreds of images of St. Anthony of Padua, the patron saint of Portugal, who was born in Lisbon, had very remarkable endowments, including surprising powers of movement. One was known to have jumped down a well in order to retrieve some stolen offerings, and it was quite a small thing that another of them should have been found weeping after the earth-

[2] The alarms were not all based on hysterical or deceitful prophecies. A Tagus pilot had observed that on the night before the great earthquake, 31 October, the turn of the tide was two hours late, and he noticed that this occurred again on 10 December, so he warned people in Lisbon that it was inadvisable to sleep indoors that night, and he was justified to the extent that there were two sharp shocks about 5 A.M. on the morning of 11 December.

quake. The renowned image of the saint in the church
of his birthplace, next to the Cathedral, with his chapel
and all its furnishings escaped the ferocious fire that burnt
out the greater part of the building, a fire so hot that it
melted the silver and bronze ornaments therein.

Many other images were miraculously preserved. A celebrated figure of Christ Carrying the Cross (Senhor dos
Passos) from the large Augustinian Convent of Graça,
crowning one of the hills on the east side of the city
(now in part a barracks), was rescued unharmed from
the church after it had been buried under fallen masonry for a week; it was an image to which the Portuguese royalties were particularly devoted, and it was dis-
interred at royal command by a party of grandess. The
image Nossa Senhora da Graça in the same church was
broken to pieces, but her head and hands survived for
making up into a new image, and a particularly celebrated crucifix was excavated unharmed. In the Church
of Nossa Senhora da Penha de França, farther to the
north, the miracle-working image of the Virgin was recovered on Sunday, the day after the earthquake, from
the ruins of the Capella Mór and displayed to the people to their great comfort and joy, and the Host was
found intact on the Monday. The image of Nossa Senhora do Carmo was rescued from the ruined convent
and set up in a tent on the Campo Grande, where it at
once became the object of fervent devotion. In the hope-
less ruins of the Franciscan church, which at the time
of the earthquake was being rebuilt after a fire, the image of Nosso Senhor dos Desemparados (Jesus of the Destitute) escaped damage, and in May 1756 a fiery sermon
was preached in a temporary wooden church erected by

the order in their *quinta* adjoining the Rato demonstrating that this astounding miracle was a sign that Our Lord had not deserted the Portuguese people, even in the hour of bitter punishment with which He had chastised them. In the Igreja da Sé (the present Cathedral) a raging fire stopped suddenly on approaching the holy image of Nossa Senhora a Grande, leaving her safe with her background curtains, her rich robes, and even the flowers in her hand. Other images of the Virgin wept over ruined Lisbon, and it was said that in the Hieronymite Church at Belém the figure of Our Lady that was crouched at the foot of the Cross sunk even lower towards the ground, and, overcome with grief at the terrible punishment of the Lisbon people, cried aloud, "It is enough, my Son, it is enough." All over the afflicted areas there were many tales told of this kind, and this happened also in Spain in the towns badly hit by the earthquake. For example, at Huelva in the ruins of a convent the Host was discovered unbroken and unharmed, miraculously protected by a single tile that was able to withstand the enormous weight of broken masonry pressing down upon it.

At the time of the earthquake many people escaped into the streets clutching images of the Virgin or of the saints from which they would not under any circumstances be parted; but many of these precious domestic possessions inevitably perished in the earthquake itself and in the fire. The devotion of the Portuguese to the figures in their private oratories was not much less than that paid to the celebrated miracle-working images in the churches, and they lived with these domestic lares on the most loving and intimate terms; in fact, they inflicted little punishments on some of them if they were unduly slow in answering prayers. Figures of Lisbon's patron saint, St. Anthony, had a specially close connexion with the household fortunes, as he was charged with the duty of recovering anything that was lost, and it was not uncommon for his image to be reproached by being bound with ribbons, or put into the corner, or banished to a dark cellar, or even suspended in the garden cistern under threat of immersion. Whenever what was lost was found, the saint was restored in honour to his proper place, and there was a little family celebration.[3]

The destruction of so many of these household images was, in relation to the damage done in the churches, a very small matter, but it added to the general religious discomfort and unsettling of a naturally pious folk, and increased their consciousness of the earthquake's supernatural significance. How long, after the first terror was over and there had been some time for reflection, the wretched people continued to feel keenly that a sinful Lisbon had been punished by God, there is now no means of telling, and several writers allege rather bitterly that the determination to lead a reformed and pious life evap-

[3] The Chevalier de Oliveira (*see* p. 155) says this was the custom in his mother's house, and he described how he himself treated his own two favourite images of St. Anthony and St. Gonzales de Amarante when these two saints, being occupied with other matters, would not soften the heart of a girl with whom he was in love; they went into disgrace under his bed and finished up in the water tank, and would have been drowned if the young lady had not unexpectedly saved them by writing the Chevalier an encouraging letter. He said he had a friend who possessed an image of St. Anthony with a movable head, and if the saint did not grant the favours required, the image's head was twisted round so that he could not see the child Christ in his arms, and this treatment nearly always produced results; but the best way to make St. Anthony answer prayers, said the Chevalier, was to take the infant Jesus out of his arms. He could never bear that punishment for long. F. Xavier de Oliveira, *Amusement périodique*, I, pp. 347-57. London, 1751.

orated very quickly indeed; but this was not for lack of chiding, and we know that in the days following the earthquake and for many months afterwards the people were constantly reminded by repeated earthquake-shocks of their danger, and in sermons and pamphlets of their wickedness and of the justice of the city's fate.

In Lisbon the frantic preaching and exhortations began almost at once after the earthquake, but the catastrophe itself was of such a kind that official gestures of repentance on a large scale could not be arranged until nearly a fortnight had passed. There were, however, two solemn penitential processions organized by the Patriarch with the approval of the King, one on Sunday, 16 November, and the other on 13 December, a Saturday, exactly six weeks after the disaster. They took place on the western outskirts of the city, well away from the congested ruins of the central burnt-out area, starting at the Ermida de São Joachim in the Alcântara district, a recent building that had escaped harm and was temporarily a headquarters of the staff of the displaced Patriarchal Church, and proceeding thence up the hill to the church of the Palace of the Necessidades. The King and Queen and the princesses took part in the first. After the second procession, attended by all the leading ecclesiastical and civic officials, there was a ceremony of footwashing conducted by the Papal Nuncio and the Oratory Fathers. A large number of the monastic establishments that had not been put completely out of action by the earthquake organized processions of their own. One arranged by the Theatine Fathers of the ruined Convento de Nossa Senhora da Divina Providéncia (also known as the Convento dos Caetanos) took place on the Campo Grande,

where the order had an *hospício,* on a dark stormy evening after incessant rain, those taking part trudging bare-
foot through the mud and puddles.

Lisbon, the people were told, had been a very sinful
city indeed. It was greedy, devoted to material wealth,
immoral, licentious, and irreverent, the behaviour in some
of the churches being, it was alleged, outrageously scandalous. For permitting this misuse of sacred buildings, the
clergy had to, and did, take their share of the blame, and
in doing so they were able to explain why God in His
anger had destroyed so many churches, great and small,
for in His disgust God had been forced to the extreme
course of abandoning His own altars, even as once long
ago He had for somewhat similar reasons (Hophni and
Phineas are mentioned as relevant examples of evil-doers)
allowed the Ark of the Covenant to be captured by the
Philistines. In no other way could the Almighty prove the
really terrible nature of His anger. Thus, it was understandable that God should not only have destroyed His
own churches, but have spared a street full of brothels;
for God pitied the miserable creatures that frequented
such places, but could not pardon those who profaned
the buildings set apart for the worship of Himself and
for the religious instruction of the faithful. This theme
was elaborated again and again, and is also to be found
in many of the earthquake sermons outside Portugal. The
Archbishop of Mexico, for instance, spared his own clergy
nothing in his pastoral letter of March 1756. Hophni and
Phineas again; allegations that church funds were mis-
used; the churches themselves used as shops and as places
for making love; it was indeed to be expected that in

Central America, just as in the Old World, God would strike these polluted temples crashing to the ground.

The classic example of the way in which God has thus pointedly expressed his displeasure was provided by Seville. After the earthquake on 1 November the Cathedral had had to be evacuated, and its dearly loved image, Maria Santísima de la Sede, removed, and it was not until 28 February 1756 that Our Lady returned to her shrine in great pomp and with much rejoicing, on which occasion a ferocious sermon was preached by a renowned orator, a canon of the Cathedral, Francisco Joseph de Olazával y Olayzola, one that is outstanding in interest even in a comprehensive survey of the remarkable earthquake-sermons of that time. Why had they all, with their beloved image, to go into exile, he asked? Here was a second cleansing of the Temple, and one only too well deserved. There had been deplorable and scandalous misbehaviour within its holy precincts; that was why, though their protectress the Virgin had seen to it that God did not wreak a full vengeance on the city over which she presided, the Almighty had spoken His mind in an unmistakable way by striking at the Cathedral and its famous tower, the Giralda, leaving the rest of the city more or less unharmed. A victory over the Church for the secular buildings of Seville! The Audiencia, the Ayuntamiento (Town Hall), and the Casa Lonja (Exchange) had all escaped without damage, and indeed the town had on the whole suffered very little and there had been very few casualties. It was the Cathedral that was the special object of God's anger. In view of the deplorable misdemeanours Olazaval mentioned in considerable detail, his

case was obviously a strong one; but the congregation no
doubt knew that the Canon's standards for behaviour in
church were exceptionally high. Within the choir and
sanctuary, he insisted, no mundane thought at all is per-
missible, and he told his hearers of the sad lapse of the
seventeenth-century Juan de Palafox, Bishop of Osma,
who so far forgot himself as to want to know the time,
the worldly time, when taking part in a service in the
choir of his Cathedral in order to keep an appointment
elsewhere that was a proper part of his pastoral duties.
He felt for his watch, but it was not in his pocket, and
he thought he must have left it at home. When he was
leaving after the service he put his hand in his pocket
again, and there was the watch. God had miraculously
removed it and replaced it, in order to teach him that
no worldly consideration at all should have entered his
mind while he was engaged in his devotions.

Some of the clergy did try hard to discourage this dol-
orous harping on the sins of the time and the accompanying warnings of dreadful punishment that might still fall
on the sinners; for instance, in Lisbon a Franciscan, F.
António de S. José, who had worked in India, seeing what
were likely to be the undesirable effects of this continual
hullabaloo about the city's wickedness, published a tiny
pamphlet which he described as a *Discurso Morál,* and
in this he wisely distinguished between teaching folk to
fear God and alarming them into downright panic. God
is close to a penitent person, he said, and does not desire to hurt him. There was no real reason to suppose
that Lisbon was going to suffer another great earthquake.
And so on.

But other preachers tried to show that all things considered Lisbon had got off lightly. This was a mistake. The people, in spite of all the rantings on the contrary side, were not persuaded that the punishment inflicted was *less* than the wicked city of Lisbon deserved; they thought, knowing that there was a very large number of ordinary good men and women in Lisbon, to say nothing of a great many innocent children, that Lisbon had suffered *more* than it deserved. The truth is that the Lisbon earthquake had forced many of the survivors and those that sympathized with them to ask themselves if God really was a loving Father. It was a question asked with greater insistence outside Portugal; but it was asked in Lisbon too, and it was one to which, under the painful circumstances of an earthquake of great severity, the clergy did not find it easy to give a convincing affirmative answer.

In this context a sermon preached fifteen months after the earthquake in a temporary church of the Franciscans in Campolide, a high outlying district in north-west Lisbon, is of great interest. The preacher called it an *Exhortação consolatoria de Jesus Christo,* and it was published in the spring of 1757, a time when Lisbon was already making a strong recovery, both in rebuilding and in commerce, and there were justifiable hopes that the city would later on be completely restored to its former prosperity. It was a time in which it was appropriate to assess the whole tragedy of the earthquake in retrospect, and to sum up its spiritual significance. The preacher was António do Sacramento, and his address took the form of an imaginary speech by Jesus Himself to a congregation consisting of the entire Portuguese nation. The text put into the mouth of Our Lord was:

O my people, what have I done unto thee? and wherein have I wearied thee? testify against me. (Micah vi. 3.)

Jesus said that the Portuguese nation might be proud to think that its people were specially singled out, above all other nations, as the object of His love. The earthquake, always remembering that God's wisdom is beyond the comprehension of men, was an act of love, not just a chastisement; for its purpose was to bring Portugal, as a beloved child, back into the comforting arms of Jesus Himself. Portugal had indeed been sinful, and Our Lord had been deeply offended; but, even so, the punishment He had inflicted had been relatively light. Just think, for instance, what the Flood must have been like! Portugal really deserved to be swallowed up completely and all its people sent to eternal damnation. Jesus had therefore been most merciful, sparing the lives of most of the city's inhabitants. He had not wanted to scare the Portuguese out of their wits, for that was not His loving way of dealing with mankind; but He had wanted to prevent His chosen people from further foolishness and to change their hearts. It was true that they had suffered; but Jesus had suffered much more horribly Himself in His Passion. If someone lost a fortune in the earthquake, it was because men must learn somehow or other not to overrate riches. Those who lost their lives were lucky people, the recipients of Our Lord's special favour, for they died quickly and mercifully, unburdened by all the sins they would have committed had they lived. The Portuguese were recommended to read Isaiah xxix and Revelation xviii if they were in any doubt about the justice of the earthquake, or were deluded by philosophers into thinking it was merely a natural accident. There must be no mistake on this point, and Lisbon, the modern Babylon, could, and perhaps should, have been destroyed like Sodom and Gomorrah. The Portuguese must try to recognize what Jesus had done for Portugal. He had made it a world power, a State universally feared for its strength, wealth, and far-flung dominions. It was Jesus who had rescued the Portuguese from the Spanish usurpation. Jesus had lived on earth, had been a man, and knew how to establish a nation in security. The Portuguese must stop lamenting, and trust in Him. The earthly punishments He inflicted were no more than the corrections of a loving father, and not the sentences of an angry judge. Come again into my arms, said Jesus.

Today this sounds at least ridiculous, if not actually blasphemous, but António do Sacramento was sincere in thus presenting to the people what was intended to be an acceptable theodicy, a justification of the God who had —it seemed so cruelly—hurt them. And in his ardent out-pouring of comfortable words we can see the theodicy taking shape. The reason why God had overthrown Lisbon was not only because He intended to shock the whole of Christendom into a state of penitent obedience to Him by the staggering destruction of such a celebrated and wealthy city, one that was perhaps, thanks to its maritime trade, the best-known city in Europe; but also because Portugal was a kingdom under the special and principal care of Heaven, so that according to the rules of the divine discipline, the Portuguese, for their own good and as a result of the heavenly priority that was their due, were singled out for the honour of being the

I. Earthquake fright in London, 1750: a satirical print

II. Lisbon before the earthquake: part of the Royal Palace and Terreiro do Paço

The central building is the Torreão do Forte built for Philip II of Spain; it was on the west side of the present Terreiro do Paço, opposite the statue of José I, the waterfront being now much farther to the south than that shown in the engraving. The building to the left on the Tagus is the palace of the Côrte Real family. This and the Royal Palace were both destroyed.

III. The Lisbon Earthquake, by João Glama Stromberle

Oil-painting, 1.5 m. x 2.4 m. Second half of eighteenth century. The scene is the Praça de Santa Catarina on high ground close to the Tagus in south-west Lisbon.

IV. The Praça de Patriarcal after the earthquake

Engraving by J. P. Le Bas, published in his *Collecção de algumas ruinas de Lisboa* or *Receuil des plus belles ruines de Lisbonne*, Paris, 1757: from drawings by MM. Paris et Pedegache. As the romantic French title suggests, these sketches are fancifully picturesque and have little documentary value. In this sketch the building on the left is a northern extension of the Royal Palace, and the observer is in the present Largo do Pelhourino (Praça do Municipio) looking north-west.

V. Lisbon *c.* 1785: detail from a map by A. F. Tardieu

The stippled area showing the Pombaline rebuilding corresponds closely to the area of the great fire after the earthquake.

VI. The Marquês de Pombal

Engraving by J. F. Beauvarlet after the painting by Louis Vanloo and Joseph Vernet. Second half of eighteenth century. The original, formerly in the possession of the Pombal family, is now the property of the Câmara Municipal de Oeiras.

In the collection of L. C. G. Clarke, Esq.

VII. Voltaire. Poème sur le désastre de Lisbonne

(Left) Opening lines of a manuscript copy sent by Voltaire to the Comte d'Argental

(Right) Accompanying letter in the hand of Voltaire, dated 19 December 1755

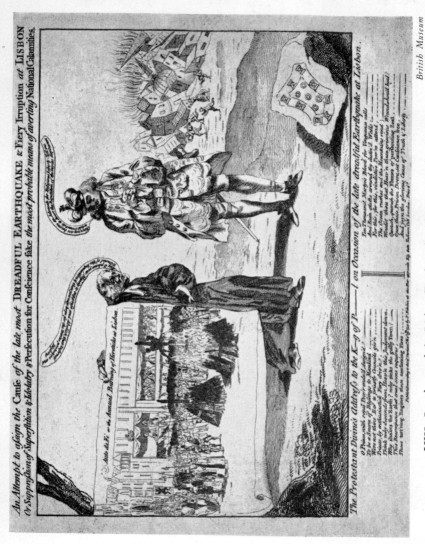

British Museum

VIII. London and the Lisbon Earthquake: the Inquisition blamed
A print published in November 1755

first to be punished and those who were punished most severely. The warrant for this heavenly favouritism, to which the opening passage of António do Sacramento's sermon alludes, was the message delivered by Christ Himself in a vision vouchsafed to the first King of Portugal, Afonso Henriques, on the eve of his famous victory over the Moors at the battle of Ourique in 1139. After the earthquake, the Portuguese were many times reminded of the comforting relevance of this extraordinary happening, just as they were reminded of it again in the dark days of the Napoleonic oppression.

The battle of Ourique is an embarrassing subject for an historian, even without the encumbrance of a stupendous miracle. It is not known for certain where it took place, and the traditional site of the battle, near the town of Ourique in the southern end of the Alentejo province, south-west of Castro Verde on the main road to Faro, is, as most modern writers agree, probably not the real scene of the contest; at least two more likely "Ouriques" are to be found much farther north; but the Portuguese of the time of the earthquake accepted the site in the south, and there is a church at Castro Verde decorated with early eighteenth-century *azulejos* illustrating the battle and the vision. The contemporary or nearly contemporary medieval chronicles give us very little information about the actual campaign, but it seems unlikely that the victory won by Afonso Henriques was a decisive event in the war of liberation, for the Moors were fighting again north of the Tagus in the following year; Ourique did, however, have some considerable political importance. Before it Afonso Henriques was a prince; after it he styled himself King of the Portuguese. The battle was therefore a proper subject for the most highly imaginative development as a legend.

The story of the miraculous appearance of Christ at the battle of Ourique is as old as the middle of the fifteenth century, but the form in which the Portuguese knew it best was the relation of it in the *Juramento* (Oath) of Afonso Henriques, a document first published in 1602 on the authority of a manuscript discovered at Alcobaça in 1596. This manuscript was suspected to be bogus even in the seventeenth century, but its defenders were tough and numerous, and in fact, right up to and including the twentieth century, the controversy about its historical value has from time to time flared up into one of the most passionately disputed rows in Portuguese history. Anyone who doubts whether the tale was still generally believed in the middle of the eighteenth century should look at the thick harvest of pamphlets published on the subject in the middle of the nineteenth century after the historian Alexandre Herculano (1810-77) had inserted at the end of the first volume of the *História de Portugal* a seemingly inoffensive note [4] in which he referred to the story of the apparition as a fable and the Alcobaça document, by that time in the Archivo Nacional, as a forgery. He was almost overwhelmed by a raging flood of either sad or angry reproach, and was called the "Luther of the Ajuda" (he was librarian in the Ajuda palace). In the eighteenth century the tide against this honest man would have run even stronger. He would probably have been burnt. After all, as was commonly

[4] *História de Portugal,* I, pp. 486-87. Lisbon, 1846.

known, the arms of Portugal (Fig. 3), familiar and to be
seen all over the city, were visible proof that Christ's
message to Afonso Henriques had been delivered and its
commands obeyed.

In his *Juramento* Afonso Henriques swore that with his
unworthy eyes he had actually seen Jesus Christ on the
Cross. It happened this way. He was with his army on

Fig. 3. The Arms of Portugal

the plain of Ourique in Alemtejo about to fight a con-
federation of Moorish kings who opposed him with a huge
army. The Portuguese had become alarmed at the prospect of such an unequal contest, and Afonso was therefore greatly perturbed; but on opening his Bible he read
the comforting story of Gideon who, encouraged before
battle by a dream, overcame with his small force the
great army of the Midianites, and he prayed to Christ
to strengthen him and his army so that he might van-
quish the heretics assembled against him. In his sleep he,
too, had a dream and it was that an old man visited him
and promised him victory and, what is more, a vision of
Christ Himself. On waking he found that the old man of

the dream was there in real life to see him, and he repeated the two promises to Afonso, adding that Christ would look favourably on him and his royal house up to his sixteenth descendant, when the succession would fail, though, even then, Christ would continue His special protection of the Portuguese people.

The next night at an arranged signal (the ringing of a bell in the old man's near-by hermitage) Afonso Henriques left the camp by himself, taking his sword and shield, and he saw suddenly a splendour in the eastern sky, gradually growing more and more brilliant until in its centre shone out the Cross itself, floating about ten cubits height from the ground and more dazzling than the sun, and stretched on the Cross was the Lord Himself, and all around was a host of white figures, whom Afonso imagined to be angels. Flinging aside sword and shield and casting off his cloak and his shoes, he flung himself prostrate before the vision, dissolved in tears; but courage came and he cried out to Jesus, asking why the Lord showed Himself to one who believed in Him so completely and not to the heretic forces, who needed just such a vision to convince them of the truth of Christianity. In gentle tones Christ answered that His purpose was to secure the establishment of Afonso's kingdom. He would win the forthcoming battle and all others fought by him against the infidel, and Afonso's warriors would immediately beg him to assume the title of King. "I," said Christ, "am founder and bestower of kingdoms and empires, and it is my wish to create through you and your descendants an illustrious state that shall carry my name all over the world, even to the most distant nations.

And in order that your descendants may know who has
given them this kingdom, you shall take as your arms
a shield blazoned with my five wounds, the price with
which I redeemed mankind, and also with the thirty
pieces of silver, the price for which I was sold to the
Jews. Everyone will know that your kingdom is specially
dedicated to me, and it shall maintain the faith in purity
and always be notable for its piety." Afonso then asked
for a blessing on himself, his descendants, and his people, and he asked that if Christ should ever want to
punish the Portuguese, he would turn His wrath on the
King and his royal line, rather than on the people themselves. Jesus promised that He would never desert the
Portuguese.

Then Afonso returned to his captains, and it was as
Christ had said; they had recovered their courage, and
they insisted he should call himself King. And then Afonso
related Christ's promise, and swore on the Bible that the
story was true, and in token thereof he commanded that
his descendants should always bear the divinely blazoned
arms of Portugal, the *chagas* or wounds, set crosswise,
having upon them the thirty pieces of silver, and for
crest the serpent of Moses, representing Christ. All this
is set down in the famous Oath or *Juramento,* finally
drawn up at Coimbra on 29 October 1152, signed and
sealed by the King, and witnessed and sealed by a very
imposing list of people.

An exacting historian cannot be expected to like this
document. Among many reasons for doubting its authen-
ticity he would fasten on the prophecy that the royal
line would fail at the sixteenth generation, and assume

therefrom that the *Juramento* was composed after the end
of the house of Avis in 1590, for after the reign of Afonso
Henriques there were sixteen kings (Sancho I to Cardinal
Henry) before the Spanish usurpation in the reign of
Philip II; [5] but the *Juramento* was not commonly subjected to this kind of criticism, and the fact is that for
a long time it was commonly accepted as a plausible
document, one that describes with substantial accuracy a
heavenly vision that *was* seen by the first King of Portugal and a divine promise that *was* actually made. Moreover, Christ's prophecies had been fulfilled. The Portuguese had spread the Christian faith over the whole world;
they had enormous colonial possessions; Brazil with its
seemingly inexhaustible wealth was still theirs; they had
indeed reaped the benefit of Christ's gracious favour. To
settle the matter, everybody knew that the arms of Portugal were (with a simplification in the number of the
pieces of silver) exactly as Christ had ordered and as
Afonso Henriques had in consequence accepted for himself and for those who came after him.

Those, therefore, whose business it was to chide the
Portuguese people in these days of calamity used the
legend of the battle of Ourique to show that the sense
of guilt expected of so sinful a nation should be indeed
both bitter and profound. Christ's own people had failed
Him, and they on whom He had loaded His favours stood

[5] The brief reign of António I, Prior of Crato, for a few weeks in the
summer of 1580 is understandably not included. By counting all male
sons of each king up to the son that actually succeeded to the throne,
a case has been made out for supposing that the prophecy refers to the
two-year interregnum (1383-85) between Fernando, the last Burgundian
king, and the first King of the house of Avis, John I (an illegitimate son
of the Burgundian Pedro I); but the Spanish usurpation is much more
likely to be the kind of break to which the *Juramento* so anxiously refers.

now signally disgraced before all the world as principal offenders against Him, as ringleaders in sinful ingratitude.

Again and again we ask ourselves how much ordinary people listened to and were affected by these exhortations during the months following the earthquake, and at what pace and in what stages the mood of helpless surrender to fear changed to a recognition that it was a proper duty for man to show courage and try to take possession of, and repair, his ruined environment. The true state of affairs cannot now be exactly determined, but it is, however, quite certain that the continued sermonizing and reproach did have a seriously disturbing effect on the people and was a positive hindrance to recovery. One reason for saying this is that in an extreme case authority was compelled to put a stop to what was considered to be unwholesome and subversive nagging. This is the banishment from Lisbon of the Jesuit, Gabriel Malagrida, a brave, saintly, and at that time rather crazy man, whose revoltingly cruel execution in the Rossio Square in 1761, for which Pombal has been held responsible, shocked people inside and outside Portugal not much less than the news of the Lisbon earthquake itself.

Malagrida was an Italian, born in 1689, but he had become in part Portuguese as his chosen work had made him one of the most celebrated missionaries of Brazil, famous for his inexhaustible energy, the moving eloquence of his preaching, and his astonishing miraculous powers. He first went to Portugal in 1749 to ask for money to build a convent at Pará (now Belém at the mouth of the Amazon), and he was received by King João V with the honours and humble reverence that might appropriately have been paid to a reincarnation of one of the Twelve Apostles. He was present at the death-bed of the King, and the Pope, Benedict XIV, said João V was indeed fortunate to have died in the arms of this holy man. He left Portugal in 1751, after having promised to return whenever it should become necessary to prepare João V's consort, Maria Ana of Austria, for death, and it was for this purpose that he did come back to Portugal in February 1754.

Once again he had a position of dominating spiritual influence, but in the new reign his power was opposed by Pombal and the courtiers of his party, and the excessively tactless and impetuous missionary was in the end denied unrestricted access to the Queen Mother. When she died in August 1754, Malagrida depended afterwards upon the patronage of Prince Pedro, and the friendship of the Tavora family and many of Pombal's enemies at court. He still had an enormous prestige for holiness, but he was at this time a wild, white-bearded eccentric whose power resided not in his political opportunities but in his unquenchable religious candour. He was a specialist in conducting retreats, which he advocated as necessary for all, and his great hope was to supplement the existing Jesuit houses in Lisbon with another building specially set apart for the purpose.

Pombal's loathing of the Jesuits and their colossal political and educational power throughout all the Portuguese territories, especially Brazil, and their palace prestige in Portugal, had nothing to do with the earthquake; but they were even more objectionable to him after the disaster because he thought the Society was responsible for most of the alarmist preaching and frightening prophecies. Pombal wanted the 1755 earthquake written off as a natural event, and he particularly resented the mischievous warnings of an earthquake to happen on 1 November 1756; yet at the very time when these rumours, attributed to Jesuits, were circulating, Malagrida, who had already deeply offended the chief minister and must have been the most detested preacher on his list of culprits, committed in Pombal's eyes the outrageous offence of publishing in the late autumn of 1756 a pamphlet called *Juizo da verdadeira causa do terremoto*—an opinion on the true cause of the earthquake—that was obviously a printed version of the sermon he had been preaching again and again in the first months after the earthquake happened, exactly the sort of sermon that Pombal considered to be most monstrously harmful. The fame of the preacher, miracle-working, holy, passionately eloquent, and a priest with an enormous personal following, gave the little pamphlet of some thirty pages a special significance. It could not be ignored, nor could anyone fail to recognize it as a challenge to the minister himself; for Malagrida flatly contradicted Pombal's view about the natural cause of the earthquake, and then did his best to destroy the peace of mind of the people assisting in the necessary business of recovery.

Malagrida said: "Learn, O Lisbon, that the destroyers of our houses, palaces, churches, and convents, the cause of the death of so many people and of the flames that devoured such vast treasures, are your abominable sins, and not comets, stars, vapours and exhalations, and similar natural phenomena. Tragic Lisbon is now a mound of ruins. Would that it were less difficult to think of some method of restoring the place; but it has been abandoned,

and the refugees from the city live in despair. As for the
dead, what a great harvest of sinful souls such disasters
send to Hell! It is scandalous to pretend the earthquake
was just a natural event, for if that be true, there is no
need to repent and to try to avert the wrath of God, and
not even the Devil himself could invent a false idea more
likely to lead us all to irreparable ruin. Holy people had
prophesied the earthquake was coming, yet the city continued in its sinful ways without a care for the future.
Now, indeed, the case of Lisbon is desperate. It is necessary to devote all our strength and purpose to the task
of repentance. Would to God we could see as much determination and fervour for this necessary exercise as are
devoted to the erection of huts and new buildings! Does
being billeted in the country outside the city areas put
us outside the jurisdiction of God? God undoubtedly de-
sires to exercise His love and mercy, but be sure that
wherever we are, He is watching us, scourge in hand."

Malagrida reminded the people of their monstrous sins,
their wicked love for theatres, music, immodest dances,
obscene comedies, bull-fighting, and so on, and he said
how particularly distressing it was that people who ought
to know better did not mind being seen at these profane
spectacles. Lisbon's vaunted piety was a fake, a dunghill
covered with snow. Neighbouring cities, scarcely harmed,
duly performed the most severe exercises of repentance
with scourging and fasts, and were astonished that Lisbon failed to make comparable demonstrations; but Malagrida said he could forgive inadequate public and individual repentance if only the wretched Lisbon sinners
would recognize an obligation to go into retreat for six
days in a Jesuit house wherein they could be properly

instructed by expert conductors in the method of making their peace with God. People do not know anything about the mechanism of true repentance, and think that loud lamentation and ejaculatory prayers are all that is required. The Lisbon people, both ordinary folk and the leaders of society, are, frankly, irreligious. It is absolutely essential that all of them must learn that only in retreat, silent and apart, under properly qualified Jesuit instruction, could they learn the right way in which to achieve the salvation of their souls.

Mr. Marcus Cheke has rightly said that Malagrida's pamphlet put in its final and most painful form the question that post-earthquake Lisbon had somehow or other to answer. Who was right? Ought the ordinary man to try to help in the work of recovery that was directed by Pombal and executed by a diligent team of officials, aided by the army and in a large measure by the clergy themselves, or ought he to set all this miserable worldly business aside and seek in what might well be his last hours to save his soul? There must be no mistake about the seriousness or urgency of Malagrida's case. If God watched Lisbon, scourge in hand, what could anyone possibly find to do more important than to placate His wrath by the exercise of true repentance? Time was short. The people might have only weeks, indeed only days, in which to live on this earth. Could anything be more urgent at this very moment than to take a last opportunity, having deliberately set all worldly affairs aside, of preparing calmly and thoughtfully for the future life?

There is no conceivable compromise here between the men of action and the men of God. The parish priests with their loving parochial work, and the religious orders with their diligent care of wounded and homeless, were acceptable and, indeed, indispensable collaborators with civil authority; but Malagrida, and those who preached like him, were undermining the patient work of these men. His accusation came very nearly to the charge that the people were being misdirected and deprived of the proper opportunity of saving their souls. He made no attempt to seek some kind of middle course. He preached his impassioned doctrine wherever he found opportunity, insisting on the absolute necessity for meditation in retreat; he sent copies of his pamphlet to members of the royal family, and to Pombal himself and other high officers of state. He became in official eyes a public menace, and Pombal, understandably angry, persuaded the Papal Nuncio to banish his troublesome countryman from Lisbon, which Filippo Acciaiuoli obligingly did, sending him into retirement at Setúbal, where he had already been residing and was occupied with the planning of a nunnery, made possible by a bequest from the late Queen.

Banishment to Setúbal did not end the nuisance caused by Malagrida and his objectionable pamphlet. He conducted retreats for both men and women, boasted of the number of souls he was saving from Hell, and continued his stormy exhortations, wild prophesying and terrifying revelations, all justified in his view by persistent supernatural promptings. Moreover, he was soon in very serious trouble, the cause being the supposed attempt of 3 September 1758 on the King's life, as letters of his written after the event for Brazil came into the hands of Pombal, and it was discovered that before the shooting he had prophesied that harm was likely to befall José I. Probably he had nothing to do with the actual occur-

rence, but Pombal had now everything he wanted for the
final attack on this very nearly crazy saint. He was put
into prison in December 1758, and the case against him
was made to appear so bad that three years later in his
obituary notice it was said of him in the *Scots Magazine*
that he "had rendered himself very famous for the deep
concern he had in the plot for assassinating his Portuguese Majesty." He escaped condemnation with the Tavora family; but he was not allowed to leave the country when the Jesuits were expelled. Instead, Malagrida
was handed over to the Inquisition by whom he was sen-
tenced in January 1761 as a heretic, on charges that he
had recently written certain blasphemous and painfully
disgusting books, full of details about the uterine life of
St. Anne, the Virgin, and Our Lord, that he had uttered
false prophecies and had pretended to have converse with
spirits, and that he had behaved with gross indecency in
prison—of which charges it can be said that, if true, they
merited no more in the way of punishment than the merciful condemnation of a lunatic to a madhouse; but Malagrida was found guilty,[6] and on the night of 21 September 1761 he was put to death by strangling in horrid pub-
licity in the torchlit end of an auto-da-fé in the Rossio
Square that had lasted all day. As soon as he was dead
his body was burnt and the ashes were thrown into the
sea. He was seventy-two.[7]

[6] An account of the trial was published in English. *Proceedings and
Sentence of the Spiritual Court of Inquisition of Portugal against Gabriel
Malagrida, Jesuit.* London, 1762.

[7] This was not the end of the *Juizo da verdadeira causa do terremoto*.
The pamphlet still circulated and troubled the conscientious reader, and
long after the wretched author had been put to death, it was found necessary to publish a royal decree banning the work as heretical. The text
of this decree, undated, is given in the *Mémoires du Marquis du Pombal*, IV, p. 247 (1784). In the text, p. 37, the suggestion is that it was
published ten years after the execution, i.e. in 1771.

Chapter Five

THE WRATH OF GOD (2)

God in His anger had destroyed Lisbon. It was a constant theme in sermons, tracts, and moralizing poetry, throughout all Europe.

> Je reconnais, hélas, à ces terribles coups,
> Un maître, un juge, un Dieu qu'anime son courroux.

So wrote the Chevalier Joseph Cuers de Cogelin, and the charitable way of explaining God's terrifying punishment within the limits of a short poem was to say that Lisbon had been too proud—mistress of the seas, a world market controlling vast possessions abroad, stupendously wealthy. Now, poetically at least, there is nothing left of this magnificent city.

> Où te trouver, lieu plein de charmes,
> Cité de mes Rois, de mes Dieux?
> Est-ce le voile de mes larmes
> Qui te cache à mes tristes yeux?

A Portuguese refugee from the ruined city is imagined by a Bordeaux poet as addressing thus the site where Lisbon had once stood. The poor wretch can only wish that he too had been killed:

Flamme infernale et souterreine,
Je vis encore, rallume toi.
Mer dévorante, qui t'arrête?
O Ciel! brise toi sur ma tête,
Tombe, fond sur elle en éclats;
Et toi, grand Dieu, vengeur du crime,
Sauve ta dernière victime
De l'horreur de ne mourir pas.

The downfall of pride is the theme of a little fable in verse written by the Abbé J. L. Aubert. He describes an ants' nest, a complacent and thriving community for whom everything seemed to go well, so much so that they accepted all the gifts of Heaven as their proper due and never bothered to be grateful to their Creator; but one day the wind shook an acorn down on the nest and it killed several of the ants. The rest of them, terrified by this awful event, regarded the calamity just in the same way as we should regard an enormous and widespread earthquake, and their pride and self-satisfaction vanished at once, for they knew now that their lives depended on the goodwill of God, and that henceforth they must be truly thankful for all the blessings they received and fear the just anger of God:

Ce que les dons du Ciel n'avoient pu sur leur cœur,
Un coup de vent en eut l'honneur.

We men and women, the Abbé observed, are insignificant little creatures just like the ants, and we behave in just the same ungrateful way. We do not give proper thanks for the abundant gifts we receive from Heaven and it is only an unexpected disaster like an earthquake that succeeds in humbling our wicked pride.

It may, however, have been pride in a curious form that brought all this suffering on the people of Lisbon; for one view was that they ought to have been living somewhere else, since they were greatly to blame for not heeding the plain warning given them by the awful earthquake that overthrew their city on 26 January 1531. They should have recognized that they lived on a site under which lurked most potent subterranean fires that had obtained means of access to the surface, so that at any time they might explode again with shattering violence, just like an enormous sapper's mine destroying a fortification. But the Portuguese persuaded themselves into a false security, and lead astray by a deep love for their charming flower-bedecked country, they failed to recognize what a dangerous place it was. In a little while unhappy Lisbon would doubtless be rebuilt again. But there was a strong probability that in due course God would destroy it once more with a third earthquake.

In most of the quickly produced poems and tracts that have as their theme the wrath of God, the writers seldom reminded their readers that God also loved His children. When God's love is mentioned, it is often somewhat grudgingly done, sometimes with a hint of reproach. A typical poem of the kind that does at least remember the sacrifice of the Son of God is one by the Abbé de St. Martin de Chassonville, who had been at Madrid in the household of the Portuguese diplomat Mendonça Côrte Real, and at the time of the earthquake was in the service of his son, Diogo de Mendonça Côrte Real, the foreign minister of King José whom Pombal was so soon to remove from office. Most of the poem is about

God's anger and the terrible punishment recently visited
on mankind; but it finishes with a prayer:

> Assez de ta juste colère
> Nous avons senti les effets;
> Daigne te montre notre Père,
> DIEU vangeur, donne-nous la paix.
> Tu nous a fait à ton image,
> Reçois nos voeux, et notre hommage,
> Finis notre calamité:
> Prens le Sang de ton Fils pour gage,
> Il nous en a permis l'usage
> Quand nous implorons ta bonté.

But all this kind of simple thought about the wrath
of God, and it can be multiplied over and over again in
only slightly divergent forms, is small conventional stuff
compared with the ferocious broodings of the men who
really did believe that the Lisbon earthquake was a heavenly punishment directed against special enormities of sin
that now at last stood exposed in their true nature to an
abashed and conscience-stricken world. A horrifying example of this sort of interpretation of the earthquake is
given us by a Jansenist, Laurent-Etienne Rondet (1717-
85), a Parisian who eventually made a small name for
himself as a Biblical scholar of formidable industry and
erudition, and also as editor of the Abbé Racine's *Abrégé
de l'Histoire ecclésiastique*. When he was a young man
he had studied under the much-respected Charles Rollin
(1661-1741), the historian of the ancient world and a
famous educationalist, who had suffered for his Jansenist
views by being deprived of the rectorship of the College
de Beauvais of Paris University while Rondet was still a

child. His thought was therefore embittered by this and no doubt other instances of the persecution of his co-religionists, and the fact that he belonged to a party labelled as heretics and regarded as enemies of the State.

Of the majority of his party it could be said that they were really very ordinary French citizens, and wanted to be nothing else, and that they desired to be peaceable members of the Roman communion; but their unforgivable faults in high places were that they were bitter opponents of the Jesuits, the most dangerous enemies that could be found against them in the religious world, and also that their conscience forced them to challenge certain aspects of the Pope's sovereignty; doctrinally they erred, or were told that they erred, in preferring the Calvinistic severities of St. Augustine's teaching on grace to the much more lenient Jesuit teaching. They were above everything God-fearing folk, many of them noble in thought and saintly in character; but there was a hard puritanical element in the make-up of some of them, and Rondet was a man in whom this was developed into a totally unsympathetic and unloving hatred of the enemies of his faith. Those enemies had indeed been active in the last years of Louis XIV. The Jansenist headquarters, the Convent of Port Royal des Champs in the country south-west of Paris, had been savagely obliterated, its occupants dispersed as prisoners, and even the graveyard cleared of its bodies; and after this Jansenism had again incurred papal condemnation through the issue of the Bull *Unigenitus* [1] in 1713.

[1] The Bull takes the form of a condemnation in various terms of 101 propositions in the *Moral Reflexions on the New Testament* by Pasquier Quesnel, first published in 1671. Only twelve of these are actually described as heretical.

By the time Rondet wrote his book on the Lisbon earthquake it was amid a storm of troubles that were good reason for the bitterness in what he had to say; yet it is also true that his message has at the same time a sinister exultant note. The Bull *Unigenitus* had had results far exceeding the intentions either of Pope Clement XI, who did not want to persecute the Jansenists, or of Louis XIV, who certainly did; the Bull had, in fact, caused a deeply felt quarrel that came near to being a schism between the French and Roman communions, and also such serious political tension that it has been held to be in some measure responsible for the French Revolution. To the Jansenists the doctrines implied by the condemnations of the Bull were denied in the Bible and in the teaching of St. Augustine; but it was generally recognized at once that, whether this were so or not, the condemnations in *Unigenitus* far exceeded a reasonable denunciation of the central Jansenist faith, and many Frenchmen without any Jansenist sympathies hated the Bull as intolerable interference with their own religious practice and belief. Led by some of the bishops and large numbers of clergy, there was a strong Gallican protest against the attempt of the Pope to force by such means as this doctrinal instruction on the French Church, and there was talk of an appeal to a General Council of the Church; *Unigenitus* was, in short, denounced with considerable popular support as ultramontanism of the most flagrant kind, and it led to so sharp a quarrel with the Vatican that the principal protesting bishops were excommunicated. But the Bull had also very powerful friends in high places in addition to the assiduous support of the Jesuits, and in 1730 it became the law of France. This was followed by public scandals, above all by passionate protests against official interference with the common right to the sacraments, especially extreme unction; at the same time the Jansenists were becoming a worse nuisance, for the miracles of the St. Médard graveyard in the Quartier Latin were followed by the hysterical performances of the convulsionaries, whose fantastic behaviour and apocalyptic denunciation of *Unigenitus* as the apostasy heralding Antichrist made it necessary to close the cemetery in 1732. *Depar le Roi, Defense à Dieu, De faire Miracle, En ce Lieu.*

On the whole the Jansenists got unexpected sympathy. By the time of the earthquake there had been riots in Paris, as a result of what seemed to be a cruel and quite unnecessary heresy-hunt, while the King was openly quarrelling with the magistrates and the Paris Parliament about the enforcement of the Bull as law. Jansenism had now acquired a political virtue, as though its main tenet were the liberty of the subject, and in these circumstances a fanatical Jansenist like Rondet saw the hand of God crushing the enemies of his faith. The Lisbon earthquake, he believed, was the final and unmistakable denunciation of these enemies before all Christendom, that is, if men would only read the signs of Heaven aright, signs that Rondet now felt it was his duty to explain to all who would read his book.[2]

[2] The book, over seven hundred pages in length, is in two parts, *Réflexions sur le Désastre de Lisbonne.* En Europe. Aux dépens de la Compagnie, 1756, pp. xi, 543, and *Supplément aux Réflexions sur le Désastre de Lisbonne,* 1757, pp. lxii, 216, with preface dated 18 April 1757. "Au dépens de la Compagnie" probably means that the publication was paid for out of a Jansenist secret fund (the Boîte à Perette) that had been founded in the seventeenth century in order to maintain the fight against the Jesuits by publications and to provide support for their Jansenist

Rondet knew that when God strikes, He strikes hard. Therefore it is useless to waste time on any unrealistic lamentation or squeamish pity for the supposedly innocent sufferers in a divine punishment of this kind. Necessarily, the just are struck down in company with the unjust. What, after all, does it matter? Everybody has got to die sooner or later, and we are all of us sinners, even little children. There is no need to worry about the death of comparatively virtuous people. The really terrible thing is that sudden death means the eternal damnation of the hardened sinner. This awful thought should make us understand and abjectly dread the colossal punishment that God inflicts upon mankind in a disaster of this magnitude.

Monsieur Rondet made two points that gave him a special advantage in studying divine retribution. The first is that God's punishment may be inflicted a long time, perhaps several hundred years, after the sinning that angered God took place, and the second is that this punishment, whenever it may be inflicted, is not necessarily inflicted upon the actual place where the offence was committed. God is patient. He told Abraham that the Amarites would wait for four hundred years before the Israelites inflicted on this wicked tribe the punishment intended for them. Again, the evil done by Manasseh, King of Judah, was remembered and punished in the reigns of his great-grandson and great-great-grandson, without any allevia-

---

victims. The phrase is often used on Jansenist title-pages with the false imprints of Cologne or Utrecht. Rondet's edition of the Abbé Racine's *Abrégé de l'Histoire ecclésiastique* is an example. The *Réflexions sur le Désastre de Lisbonne* is probably a Paris book, and from the same press as the 1748 and 1752 editions of the *Abrégé*. I have to thank my colleague Mr. A. F. Allison for giving me this information.

tion on account of Manasseh's reported repentance or of the religious reformation carried out by his grandson Josiah; for the fall of Jerusalem in 597 B.C. and the subsequent captivity were both the consequences of the wickedness of Manasseh, who died about 641 B.C. And we learn from this particular example that God does not always punish in one decisive blow the people who have angered Him; *il les frappe par degrés*, said Rondet; thus Nebuchadnezzar had to attack Jerusalem three times before he succeeded in destroying the city and burning the Temple. There are many other examples of this kind of delayed and protracted punishment. The destruction of Jerusalem in A.D. 70 and the Hadrianic banishment of the Jews were punishments for the Crucifixion. The schismatic Greeks were punished in the fifteenth century for sins dating back to the ninth century. Then, as regards place: note that the penal earthquakes following the Crucifixion took place in Asia Minor and not in Judaea; similarly, earthquakes of about A.D. 468 in the Dauphiné and particularly in the city of Vienne were warnings of disasters about to fall on Rome in the period from the revolt of Ricimer to the end of the Western Empire in A.D. 476. *En frappant Vienne, Dieu menaçoit Rome.*

With all this in mind, Rondet turns to the case of Lisbon. It was a busy port, a centre of commerce known everywhere in Europe, with a large population of foreigners of many nationalities; so, firstly, it is obvious that when God destroyed it by an earthquake he was addressing Himself to the whole of Europe. Next, Lisbon was the capital of Portugal, and Portugal, like Spain, is a country infamous for the severity of its Inquisition. Only a brief acquaintance with the history of this organization is needed in order to convince us that in punishing by earthquake both Lisbon and Seville, God was deliberately blasting two notorious cradles of this unholy institution.

Rondet has also another dreadful observation to make about cradles of sin; for Portugal is a cradle of the Jesuits. There was a great earthquake in Lisbon in 1531, as he had already said, in the reign of King João III, and shortly afterwards, heedless of the divine warning, the misguided King invited the Society of Jesus to Portugal; he allowed them to establish themselves at Coimbra, Evora, and Lisbon, and it was he who first sent Jesuit missionaries to Africa and Brazil. Deservedly, he died of apoplexy in 1557; his children all died at early ages, and the folly of his grandson Sebastian lost the kingdom of Portugal to Spain. The Lisbon earthquake was therefore a blow specially directed against the Jesuits; the city was the first place in which they were received with enthusiastic royal favour, and so it was God's principal target when His punishment fell upon Europe. Triumphantly, but inaccurately, Rondet pointed out that all the seven houses of the Jesuits in that city had been destroyed, and he noted a report in the papers that the original Jesuit College at Coimbra had also been damaged.

The case against Lisbon was not, however, yet complete; it was also the cradle of Molinism, for the Spanish Jesuit, Luis de Molina, published in Lisbon in 1588 his *Concordia liberi arbitrii cum gratiae donis*, etc., a celebrated reconciliation of free will and predestination through grace that occasioned a major theological controversy and was a principal object of Jansenist hate. Finally, added to this pile of Lisbon wrongdoing, was the scandal of the Laxist Casuists, whose deplorable, indulgent moral code was the product, according to Rondet, of Portugal when united with Spain as one kingdom. The Jesuit Francisco Suárez, a most celebrated Spanish scholar, was involved in this perversion of moral theology, and it could be said against him that he was a professor at Coimbra for nineteen years and that he died in Lisbon (1617). There was no room left for doubt. A Jansenist of Rondet's sort knew that Lisbon was doctrinally damned.

The whole matter is made worse by the timing and manner of the earthquake, for there are ways in which God adds special emphasis to His awful message. By destroying Lisbon at a popular time for Mass on a solemn festival, God condemned the general disgracefully irreverent attitude to His services and holy days, and in choosing All Saints' Day, God made known that it was the saints themselves who had begged Him to punish Lisbon; because of its wickedness they had cried to Him, "How long, O Lord, holy and true, dost thou not judge and avenge our blood on them that dwell on the earth?" [3] Then, again, the disaster took place at Terce, the hour when the Church daily remembers the descent of the Holy Ghost at Pentecost, the great gift of grace which Molina and the Jesuits so shockingly misunderstood, which even popes had shamefully insulted in outrageous briefs and bulls.

A Jansenist's deepest feelings are now roused. Is it possible that there is a connexion between the Lisbon earthquake and the infamous destruction of the beloved Con-

[3] Revelation vi. 10.

vent of Port Royal des Champs on 29 October 1709? The vile act began with the forcible removal of the nuns between Terce and Sext on that day, and it was reported to the prefect of police as completed on All Saints' Day; everyone knew the subsequent fate of the buildings and the graveyard. The dust of this holy house, said Rondet, demands vengeance, and now already we see that God is striking a city that first fostered Port Royal's most bitter enemy, the Jesuits. We are to note here that the Lisbon earthquake happened precisely 150 years after the shameful refusal of Pope Paul V to issue a Bull denouncing Molina, the cowardly act that was the source of all the subsequent troubles in the Church.

Molinisme! This scandalous doctrine must be the plague of locusts of Chapter 9 of the Book of Revelation that had power to hurt men for "five months," an expression that may mean 150 years, since the Biblical "day" often means a year, and $5 \times 30 = 150$. St. John goes on to say that "one woe is past; and behold, there come two woes more hereafter," and with this clue, being sure enough that Molinism must be the first woe, the full meaning of the vision of the seven angels can be explained in terms of familiar Church history. The Lisbon earthquake is the trumpet of the sixth angel announcing the sixth plague, which is the second woe that is soon to fall upon us. It is also highly probable that Molinists are prophetically denounced in the four plagues of Joel (i. 4) for the palmerworm, the locusts, the cankerworm, and the caterpillar, refer (among other things) to the four major appearances of false teaching in the Western Church, namely the Albigensian heresy, the influence of Wycliffe and Hus, the heresies of Luther and Calvin, and the Molinists, obviously the caterpillars. Now, of these, the first three have been decisively punished, so it is alarmingly probable that the Lisbon earthquake is the warning of a terrible fourth punishment that will soon astound the world. Whatever form it may take, it will be something very terrible, comparable perhaps with the punishment the Greek Church received for its act of schism, that is, conquest by Islam. Joel said, "Alas for the day! for the day of the Lord is at hand, and as a destruction from the Almighty shall it come." [4]

This summary has not yet taken us a quarter way through all that Rondet has to say. The whole of the events connected with the earthquake had also to be discussed in relation to Biblical prophecy. The shocks felt in Africa show that God is also threatening Islam; hitherto He used the Mohammedans as a rod whereby to scourge the Christians; but, as Jeremiah foretold, the rod itself shall be broken.[5] We are told why earthquakes have lately alarmed both North and South America, and also Kaschan in Persia, Constantinople and Cairo; but here let us leave Monsieur Rondet and his loveless unsympathetic book. He had no sorrow for the sufferers; it was in his eyes right that men, women, and children should die miserably, crushed by blow after blow falling everywhere on the earth from the scourge of an angry God. Blow after blow dealt regularly throughout all history whenever men have erred. Rondet knew that men must cringe without protest under the painful flogging they had so richly deserved. Would that eighteenth-century sinners had something of the wisdom and piety of

[4] Joel i. 15.
[5] Cf. Jeremiah xxv. 9-12.

their forefathers; they did at least pay attention to the
dreadful signs of divine wrath; they winced under God's
chastisement dreading an even worse punishment, which
was, it is unhappily true, usually their fate. How different it all is now! How little the Lisbon earthquake
really means to us!

We cannot say that the Chevalier de Oliveira was unloving and had no sorrow for the sufferers in the earthquake. He was a Portuguese living in exile in London,
and his grief on hearing of the disaster that had befallen
his dear country, where his family lived and he still had
many friends, was obviously sincere. "With how many
tears have I not bedew'd the Paper, on which I write
the Name of my August afflicted Sovereign, and those of
my near Relations, my ancient Friends, and, in one word,
of all the Portuguese?" [6] In England he could only worry
and lament, bitterly regretful that he could not offer to
take part in the rescue work on the site; he knew that as
long as he lived he would grieve over the present afflic-
tion of Portugal and the terrible fate of the lovely city
of Lisbon. *Qui n'a pas vu Lisbonne, n'a rien vu de bon*,
it used to be said. Now there was no Lisbon.

It was in Lisbon that Francisco Xavier de Oliveira
(1702-83) was born, the son of a highly placed Treasury
official who spent much of his time abroad in the dip-
lomatic service. The son also received an Exchequer post,
and for many years afterwards he led a gay and prosperous life in Lisbon, receiving from the King in 1729
the honour of an appointment as a Chevalier of the Or-

[6] *A Pathetic Discourse*, p. 5. Second edition. London, 1756. This is a
piratical English translation of the Chevalier's *Discours Pathétique*.

der of Christ. He was a quarrelsome and profligate young man, possibly under some slight suspicion of being unorthodox in his religious views; but he married happily in 1730, and though he lost his wife three years later, he seemed to have a fine career before him when he was sent to Vienna in 1734 to replace his father, who had just died, as Secretary of the Portuguese Embassy. His stay in Austria, however, was most unhappy, for he was slighted by his chief, the Conde de Tarouca, who died suddenly at a most unfortunate moment in their relations, and in addition to a charge of treacherous conduct, he also incurred ruinous expenditure for which he considered he should have been officially reimbursed.[7] Six years later he moved to Holland, and though he claimed to have some State business there, he was now chiefly concerned with the presentation to his own government of his case for redress. He stayed in Holland until 1744, and it was in this Protestant country that he became convinced that he would be spiritually happier as a member of a reformed church than in the Roman Church in which he had been brought up. So drastically did he revolt from his former allegiance that he convinced himself that the Roman communion was in error and blinded by superstition and idolatry. For family reasons, and because he was still trying to recover his good name after the trouble in Vienna, he kept his conversion to himself for a while; but the amusing and informative books he wrote and published at this

[7] For a brief and most unfavourable account of the Chevalier de Oliveira, see Alfredo Duarte Rodrigues, *O Marquês de Pombal e os seus biógrafos*, pp. 337-38. Lisbon, 1947. This account refers indignantly to a proposal made in 1923 that one of the streets running north to south between the Rua Morais Soares and the Rua Marquês da Silva should be named after the Chevalier as one of Lisbon's distinguished literary sons.

time were indiscreetly outspoken on the subject of the
Conde de Tarouca and his family, and also on religious
matters, as one may see by reading the chapter on the
Inquisition in the first volume of his *Mémoirés . . . con-
cernant le Portugal,* and he now received a direct rebuff
from his native land because the Inquisition, probably
more for political reasons than on account of their heretical content, refused to allow these works to be put on
sale in Portugal; this caused him serious financial loss as
he had had the greatest difficulty in getting them printed.

The Chevalier de Oliveira next moved to London, still
busy with his protest against the wrong done to him in
Vienna, and here he met Senhor de Carvalho, the future
Marquês de Pombal and at that time Minister Plenipotentiary in England, who received him kindly, though he
now naturally refused to become involved in the tiresome
suit of his visitor; here, too, in 1746 he finally renounced
Rome and entered the Anglican Church under the guidance of Majendie of the Savoy Chapel, an act which,
when it became known in Portugal, naturally lost him the
little remaining sympathy of his scandalized family. However, in spite of serious financial troubles and eighteen
months' imprisonment for debt, he married for a third
time (a second wife had died in Vienna), and did a little
writing, producing in 1751 the *Amusement Périodique* in
instalments,[8] an exceedingly rare book in the diverting
gossipy style of his *Cartas Familiares,* published in Holland in 1742. The Chevalier was a witty and amusing

[8] The full title is *Oeuvres Mêlées: ou Discours Historiques, Politiques,
Moraux, Littéraires et Critiques publiés . . . sous le titre d'Amusement
Périodique.* It appeared in three volumes, January-April, May-August,
September-December. A Portuguese translation (*Recreação Periodica*)
by Aquilino Ribeiro was published in Lisbon in 1922.

man, obviously a notable and most lovable chatterbox, and these three volumes and the other works containing his table-talk are extremely entertaining; but the *Amusement Périodique* attracted little attention in England, and in Portugal it merely succeeded in angering the Inquisition further, as is understandable enough after even a short perusal of its contents. In 1753 this unfortunate man, still burdened by debts and bad health, and handicapped by the fact that he knew no English, was able to rent a tiny house in the country outside London at Kentish Town, and he was living there when the news of the Lisbon earthquake arrived.

He was dismayed and unhappy, for he loved Portugal; but he knew that he had now something very important to say to the Portuguese, so he wrote his *Discours Pathétique au Sujet des Calamités présentes arrivées en Portugal,* which was published in 1756 (price 1s.). This slim quarto volume of fifty-two pages sold so well that several reprintings were necessary, and an English translation also appeared, though the author said it was without his consent. Three copies of the French edition were sent to Portugal with letters from Oliveira, one to Dom Manuel, the King's uncle, one to Pombal, and one to the Royal Academy of History, and another copy was sent to Dona Maria Barbara, the Queen of Spain, King José's sister. The copies addressed to Lisbon arrived late in June, and by early July the Inquisition had decided to forbid the reading of the book. On 8 October an official proclamation was issued by the Holy Office in Lisbon for general distribution through Portugal condemning the *Discours Pathétique* in company with Ange Goudar's *Relation Historique* (see p. 86) and two books containing some prayers listed as forbidden on the Index, one of which was a 1753 Coimbra edition of a work by Fleury; under pain of excommunication, these works were not to be read and those possessing them were to hand the copies over to the ecclesiastical authority. It is quite plain, however, that the principal abomination denounced in this wrathful document is the "scandalous attack on our Most Holy Faith" contained in the pamphlet on the earthquake written in London by the Chevalier de Oliveira.[9]

There is nothing surprising about that. The *Discours Pathétique* is a fiercely worded direct attack on the Inquisition and the Roman Church in Portugal, and it is addressed to the King himself, for the Chevalier (Sir Francis Oliveira, as his English friends sometimes referred to him) considered himself entitled by reason of his membership of his order and his former court connexions to appeal direct to the sovereign. He said first of all that the cause of the earthquake was the anger of God, and his general reflections on this specially notable example of divine punishment are those that were expressed over and over again in the sermons and pious tracts of the time; but these simple considerations are no more than a brief introduction to his real message. He could not bring himself to believe that the Portuguese were really aware of the calamitous significance of what has happened, for surely they must see that God has angrily discontinued His former loving protection of this country.

[9] The *edital* was read publicly on Sunday, 17 October 1756 and on this occasion there was a fine display of earthquake-nerves at São Roque. After the reading and on the appearance of the Host from the ruined Church of the Encarnação, which was kept in São Roque, a woman had screaming hysterics, and this made people immediately think that an earthquake was taking place, or about to take place; so there was a stampede to get out of the church in which many people got injured.

The earthquake shows that God's grace is withdrawn. He has turned His back on the wailing petitions of the victims, because God never answers those who invoke His aid in a manner He detests. God will have nothing to do with superstition and idolatry. The Chevalier said one could certainly be thankful that the life of King José had been saved, but, having saved the King, God must now be asked to preserve the King's feet from stumbling.

Hear and assist him by thy Bounty! [the exile prayed]; add to the Days, thou hast allotted him a longer period; that he may have time to recollect his Error, and be convinced of his ill conduct; to rectify the pernicious Principles of his People, and to put an end to the Transgressions of thy holy Law; by which he and his Subjects have drawn upon them the Chastisements with which thou hast visited them in thine Anger. Yes, sir, in spite of your own heart, you are in a gross Error.

The Chevalier's case against his country is simple. First of all he denounced the idolatrous adoration of images, in his view "diabolical, infernal, and ridiculous, in all its parts." There were no greater idolaters anywhere than the Portuguese. The saints in Heaven did not expect to be infuriated by incense and prayers offered to their images; they required no more than that the living should join them in offering to God the praise and worship due to Him alone. His second charge is that the reading of the Bible is prohibited. If a legislature wanted the State they were governing to be properly and intelligently ordered, would they prohibit the reading of the Statutes of the Realm? Thirdly, and most violently, he attacked that "odious Tribunal," the Inquisition, who were deliberately responsible for the gross ignorance of the Portuguese in religious matters. Fourthly, the Chevalier considered the treatment of the Jews in Portugal to be brutal and extremely foolish. It could be easily shown that the Jews had made valuable contributions to the welfare of the country. To persecute them was politically and financially absurd. "Great King! is this the method to promote commerce, or to make arts and sciences flourish?"

The Chevalier de Oliveira at this point plunged bravely and foolishly into his final magnificent appeal. The King must reform Portugal. There was no other hope for his unhappy country. King José must put an end to the mischief caused by the Inquisition. He must rid himself of its influence, and in order to decide how best to carry out the reformation necessary if Portugal were to be saved, the King would now be well advised to invite learned theologians of other nations, especially of France and Germany, to confer with him. "Then, sir, being well instructed by yourself, of the *pro* and *con*, in this important Controversey; you could easily recline the Balance on the Side of Truth and Reason."

One might well imagine that this pamphlet was really written for a Protestant public, a timely tract that would enhance the Chevalier's reputation in the country of his adoption and prove the sincerity of so valuable a convert. Yet, it was nothing of the sort. As Professor Gonçalves Rodrigues has said,[10] there is a wild streak of vanity in Oliveira's writings suggesting that he really did think his voice would be heard with respect in his na-

[10] *Cavaleiro de Oliveira. Opúsculos contra o Santo-Ofício*, p. vi. Coimbra, 1942.

tive land, a land that was almost unapproachable and in practice unpersuadable with regard to the intimate religious matters this despised apostate in exile wished to be changed. His fantastic determination to make Portugal listen to him is proved by his next publication, the *Suite du Discours Pathétique ou Réponse aux Objections et aux Murmures que cet Ecrit s'est attiré à Lisbonne,* which he wrote in the spring of 1757 and published in that year. He had received through the many friends he still had in Lisbon a summary of, or copies of, the "odious reproaches" made against him, and these he thought it right to confute with the vigorous expostulation that is characteristic of his polemical style; he then added a criticism, absurd in its exaggeration and niggling anti-Popish stupidity of the quite sensible account of the Lisbon earthquake by António Pereira (*see* p. 91).

To show his mood the Chevalier printed a letter dated 22 December 1756 from his clerical brother in Lisbon, Tomás de Aquino, a sadly shocked Benedictine monk of high official position in his order, whose first hope was that Oliveira would disown the *Discours Pathétique,* or, if he could not do that, admit his grievous sin in having written it and return as a penitent to the Roman Church. The letter concluded by announcing that their mother had died on 24 April, perhaps Father Tomás sadly supposed, to escape the blow caused by her son's cruel humiliation of the family. To this appeal the Chevalier, though he signed himself *le frère le plus tendre et le plus affectioné,* sent back a cold uncompromising answer in a letter of 12 April 1757; he was a Protestant, he said; nothing could alter his views. He referred to the death of his mother, of which he had already been told, and to the alleged humiliation of his family that was supposed to have hastened her end. This blow to your pride, this humiliation, said the Chevalier, is not my work, but the work of God; if my relations in Portugal have suffered as a result of the views expressed in my *Discours Pathétique,* they have suffered deservedly, and no one can help them but God.

The Inquisition had not, however, finished with this rebel. On Sunday, 20 December 1761, the Chevalier de Oliveira was burnt in effigy, with his heretical book added to the bonfire, at the horrible auto-da-fé in Lisbon in which Malagrida was executed (*see* p. 141). The insult was more than he could silently endure, and he felt all the bitterness such public humiliation in his native country might be expected to cause. As a result he wrote a small book that is partly autobiography and partly a strongly worded defence of his conversion and religious convictions, *Le Chevalier d'Oliveyra brulé en Effigie: Comment et Pourquoi?* now a rare work of which there is a copy in Lambeth Palace Library, lately republished by Professor Gonçalves Rodrigues.[11] This pamphlet is also a hard and sometimes unreasonable book, of little value as a critical essay in doctrinal controversy; but it is sincere, and because of its earnest pleading it is an impressive statement of a Protestant convert's unchangeable and unappeasable hatred of the communion he had deserted. *Toutes les Religions qui employent le fer et la feu pour*

---

[11] *Opúsculos,* pp. 53 ff. The original is a small volume, 6½ × 3¾ in., of 124 pages. Printed by J. Haberhorn, Grafton Street, St. Ann's, Soho. Professor Gonçalves Rodrigues has had to reprint the text in 4°, and he has added two appropriate contemporary English engravings of an auto-da-fé and the Tavora execution, and a French engraving of Malagrida. A copy of the pamphlet has been recently acquired by the British Museum.

*contraindre les hommes à en embrasser les Dogmes, sont
certainement fausses.* That is the heartfelt beginning to
the justification of his views.

The news of the ridiculous fate of the Chevalier de
Oliveira in this auto-da-fé at Lisbon did not pass unno-
ticed outside Portugal, for it lightened with a momentary
gleam of humour the horror of the announcement of the
brutal execution of Malagrida. From a Geneva press appeared a tiny pamphlet called *Epître du Chevalier d'Oliveyra sur le dernier Acte du Foi* whose author called himself Mr. de ★★★, and in this very witty Voltairean *jeu
d'esprit,* after a devastating little preface comes a short
poem:

> O vous de la triste figure
> Preux Chevalier d'Oliveyra,
> A Lisbonne votre peinture
> Vient d'expier par la brûlure,
> Le grand scandale que causa
> La peu catholique brochure
> Que votre plume composa.

The miserable victim Malagrida is then represented as
crying out to the Inquisitors that they should think of
the taunts and reproaches the founder of his Company,
St. Ignatius Loyola, would hurl at St. Dominic, the orig-
inator of the Inquisition, when his soul arrived in Pur-
gatory. At the end of the tirade the Jesuit saint asks if
it were really necessary that Malagrida should be dispatched to his future life in the company of the effigy
of a vile renegade who was laughing at them all, Jesuits
included?

The Chevalier de Oliveira died in 1783 and was buried
in the graveyard of St. Augustine's, Hackney, close to the

present parish church, St. John's. He had tried to intervene again in Portuguese affairs in 1767, before his move to Hackney, by publishing a tiny book in Portuguese under the pseudonym of Felix Vieyra Corvina de Arcos, an anagram of his own name, the purpose of which was to praise the *Tentativa Theologica* of António Pereira de Figueiredo, whose account of the Lisbon earthquake he had so scornfully attacked in 1757; for the learned Portuguese theologian's opinions now thrilled the exiled Chevalier with hope, because this challenge to Rome and ultramontanism, coupled with the certain news of Pombal's anti-Vatican and anti-clerical policy, made him think that the religious heart of Portugal might after all be changing.[12] The Chevalier also wrote, a year later, an apocalyptic study of the reign of Antichrist in which his hatred of the Roman Church found its silliest and most bitter expression. He had written in his lighter manner on this subject in the *Amusement Périodique;* [13] but by this time he was getting old, and it is easy to think of him as a lonely disappointed man, hard-set and humourless in his views like Rondet, another authority on Antichrist. It is not fair, however, to dismiss the Chevalier too hastily. He was a failure, and his works and views attracted a very little attention in England; but he was in his prime

[12] The suggestion that this book was actually commissioned by Pombal is disproved by its contents, cf. p. 7 of these *Réflexions.* London, 1767.

[13] Tom. III, pp. 362 ff., Londres, 1751. The Chevalier tells us he commonly referred to the Bishop of Rome as Antichrist, and considered he had far better reason for doing so than the Bishop of Rome had for styling himself Pope or Universal Father; but the Pope himself is not Antichrist, even though almost everybody knows he is as much anti-Christian as Antichrist can possibly be; the Pope is only a sort of advance agent for the real Antichrist.

a most entertaining person, full of anecdotes and chatter, and with a crowd of scientific interests that he maintained throughout his life. He finished his days with only a small circle of friends, mostly members of foreign families settled in London; but they seem to have been a faithful band, and one of them, Matthew Maty, the second principal librarian of the British Museum, whose father was a Huguenot from Provence, is known to have been greatly attached to him. His obituary notice in the *Gentleman's Magazine* is that of an interesting and respected Londoner.

When Monsieur Rondet and the Chevalier de Oliveira succeeded in identifying the objects of their fiercest theological hatred among the grim portents of the Book of Revelation, they were delivering final attacks on the foe in the typical manner of their extravagant writings on the sins that had provoked God into destroying Lisbon. From such oversincere single-purposed Christians we cannot expect a thoughtful answer to the question why God had permitted this dreadful disaster to take place, nor indeed from any of the vituperative sermons preached in the churches. In contrast, therefore, let us turn thankfully to one of the men who spoke with a different and wiser voice. He is Pastor Élie Bertrand (1717-97) of the French Church in Berne. His message was bound to command attention, because he was a naturalist of some fame, and though still in the late thirties when the Lisbon earthquake took place, he was already a member of the Royal Academies of Berlin and Göttingen; moreover, earthquakes were one of his subjects, and in 1752 he had published a paper on the interior structure of earth.

Bertrand's teaching on the subject of the Lisbon earthquake is simple. It must, he said, be regarded as God's
work, and though it is no doubt part of His physical government of the earth, on which subject there is a good
deal to be said scientifically, the overriding consideration
now must be that it is also part of God's moral government of the world. Here we must stand completely
abashed by our ignorance of God's mind and purpose, and
any suggestion by us that we know why He destroyed
Lisbon is merely wicked presumption. Nevertheless, our
minds are full of this disaster, and it is right that we
should carefully discuss its theological significance; but
we must do this with theological completeness. We must,
for instance, view the Lisbon earthquake in the light of
the principal attributes of God. Thus a first certainty is
that we must fear God, for God is Holy. A wise man is
afraid of his moral judgements, and while we are on this
earth we must stand in awe of Him. "And unto man he
said, Behold, the fear of the Lord, that is wisdom; and
to depart from evil is understanding." [14] Secondly, we
must grope our way through our present alarm and grief
to a contemplation of God as immutable. Civilizations
come and go; mankind may be destroyed; even our earth
may be superseded by a new earth made for new inhabitants. But God is eternal and He is unchanging, and
it is in His everlasting unchangeable care that man will
find an ultimate restful home. Thirdly, let us be led to
the thought that God is loving. There is proof of His
bounty all around us in His created world; how quickly
we forget in our present mood of distress the overwhelm-

[14] Job xxviii. 28.

ing outpouring of benefits that He has bestowed upon us!

The pastor preached a course of four "earthquake" sermons in Berne, the first on 30 November 1755 expressly related to the Lisbon disaster, the second on 14 December on occasion of a shock that had been felt in Switzerland, the third on 28 December, and the fourth on the General Fast-Day observed in Switzerland on Thursday, 19 February 1756.[15] He came boldly and immediately to the point with his text, "And many nations shall pass by this city, and they shall say every man to his neighbour, Wherefore hath the Lord done thus unto this great city?" [16] To find an answer to this question, he said, we need first of all faith, charity, humility, and penitence. Faith because we must trust in Providence. God caused this earthquake, and however shocked we are, we must still have a complete faith in God. Charity, because we have become hard-hearted and frivolous; now we must pray that our hearts be flooded with a warm love for all our fellow-men, especially those who have suffered in the earthquake, regardless of any considerations of race, language, form of religion, or politics. Humility, because we must stop thinking that God is favouring us, and that we are a more virtuous people than those He has afflicted. Penitence, because we must all now think of death and the Last Judgement, and so consider how our lives should be immediately amended.

"Wherefore hath the Lord done thus unto this great city?" There is only one answer that man dare make, and that is that God has by this act imposed a duty on all

[15] They are published in Bertrand's *Mémoire sur les tremblemens de Terre*. Vevey, 1756.
[16] Jeremiah xxii. 8.

of us, the duty of becoming better Christians. Every line of thought about the earthquake leads to some deficiency in our conduct towards God, and so let us accept it as a signal to all of us to try to draw nearer to God, who is Holy, Immutable, and Loving.

Chapter Six

THE INJUSTICE OF GOD

One generation passeth away, and another generation cometh: but the earth abideth for ever," said the Preacher. And now after 1 November 1755 man could trust in nothing, not even in the solid earth. "O Earth," wrote the poet, "you mighty rock-like unassailable thing, is it really credible that one so strong and massive should be found to move in terrifying shudders? How can wretched man find security anywhere if the strong earth itself no longer offers security? Why do you tremble?" Alas, the poet knew the answer only too well. Earth and mankind stand in a divine relationship, for man is clay made animate. The earth from which man was made was inanimate and insensitive; but now man, the living sensitive creature, is sunk in sinful sleep, unconscious of his guilt, and it is the stolid earth, ashamed of man's lethargy, which comes to life to rouse the sleepers on its surface, to shake and terrify them, so that they may repent while it is time and save themselves. In frantic paroxysms, the earth cracks open; it cannot support further the rebellious obduracy of man, and through its opened mouths it announces with brutal emphasis that man's sins have angered God.

The sonnet *Por castigar, Senhor, nossos insultos* by Domingos dos Reis Quita and the *Parénesis* (Παραίνεσις = exhortation) *ao Terremoto* of Francisco de Pina e Mello (1695-1773) are the best known of the contemporary Portuguese earthquake-poems. The sonnet [1] says what we already know—that God flung down His own temples and reduced them to ashes rather than see them profaned by the scandalous sinners of Lisbon. The *Parénesis* is a longer poem with much more to say.

Pina e Mello [2] was born at Montemor-o-Vélho, between Coimbra and the coast, and he was living there at the time of the earthquake, a man who had already become in a minor and retired way a literary figure commanding respect. IIe had published a stout little volume of agreeable juvenilia in 1752, and in the earthquake year he printed his *Bucolica,* a set of eclogues and sonnets in what he called a rustic style, and he also wrote a long poem, *Triumpho da Religião,* that was published in 1756. It is this work that best illustrates his knowledge and powers of thought, for it has a long prologue on the nature of poetry that would be a credit to the scholarship of any land, and the *Triumpho* itself, a defence of his own orthodox Christianity against atheism, polytheism, deism, free-thinking, Mohammedanism, Judaism, and Lutherism, is a fine essay in combative argument that could only have been written by a scholar widely read in the classics, the Fathers, and in general theology and Church history. His work, however, was disliked by certain other Portuguese literary men, because it was identified with

---

[1] *Oxford Book of Portuguese Verse,* 1925. No. 156.

[2] For this poet, see António Ferrão in *Academia das Ciências de Lisboa, Boletim de 2a classe,* xx (1926-29), p. 101.

the "modern" school of French writers, which at this time meant that his recent verse was lively, sentimental, and topical.

Immediately after the earthquake, Pina e Mello delivered a most eloquent oration in the chapel of the Hospital Real at Montemor-o-Vélho to the Confraternity of Our Lady of the Conception, and his poem, the *Parénesis*, appeared in 1756. It began with an address to the fickle earth in the manner already described; and adds as a further reproach the lamentation that if, as now appeared, the divinely sponsored immobility of the earth could not be depended upon, the mad and impious Copernican theory gained some apparent and highly undesirable support; for Pino e Mello had no sympathy with or real knowledge of contemporary scientific thought in Europe, and he refused to believe, like the Bishop of Guadix and many contemporaries in Spain and Portugal, that the earth moved round the sun. Scientists, and their theories, must be denounced. The earth did not move. God had said so, and a natural explanation of the earthquake was therefore unbelievable. God made the earthquake, and was speaking to wicked mankind through this awful happening, this supremely unnatural event. And so we pass into the familiar theme of the sermons.

That much we have heard before; but there is another thought expressed in this poem. Is God really merciful? If He is, can He contemplate unmoved by tears this bitter humiliation of His people? God is the Sovereign Author of Nature, surveying and governing the huge extent of the globe from His heavenly throne; with His aid, specially promised at Ourique, He has given the Portuguese mighty dominions and has led Portuguese missionaries

into the farthest corners of the earth in order to establish
there His Church. Now He has forgotten the Portuguese
achievements in His name; He has withdrawn His protection; in contempt He has struck at the Portuguese.
Poor Lisbon! Absorbed in revelry and vice, were you
really more odious in God's sight than Nineveh? We are
told plainly enough how wicked that city was, yet God
permitted Nineveh to be given proper warning by a
prophet and a fair chance to repent! Pina e Mello now
seems too amazed by his own audacity to continue this
line of thought. How dare he presume even to try to
comprehend the divine wisdom? It is his duty to sub-
mit; groaning and tearful he must humble himself before
Providence, for he does know God can be merciful even
in His anger; but a hint of his secret indignation is blurted
out. If you are, O God, so generous and long-suffering,
admit that the earthquake was an even more severe punishment than we deserved; say, at any rate, that it is
punishment enough!

In his discourse to the Confraternity at Montemor-o-
Vélho the poet had already expressed this resentment in
a passage of dramatic eloquence. He recalls the splendid
history of his country achieved under the blessing of God
and with the help of His strong arm. And now it all
seems wasted endeavour, for if God remembered the
mighty deeds performed and the hardships endured in
His name, could He possibly be so angry with Portugal
today? Does God think the Portuguese have degenerated?
Were they not the same Portuguese to whom He made
His promise at Ourique? What is going to happen next?
May not even our Montemor-o-Vélho be doomed? Is it
not indeed likely that we shall give God further grave

offence by hardening our hearts against Him under such punishment, instead of repenting? But who are we, and who are you, O God? You are the holiest in the height, and we are poor rebels. You are firm of purpose; we are irresolute. You are unchangeable; we are inconstant and weak. And it is against such a paltry thing as man, man as powerless as an autumn leaf in the wind, that you, O God, let loose your omnipotent fury. Against man born in sin and corrupt; against man who by his very nature is inclined to do wrong. Job has said what the poet hardly dare say. If, O God, you desire greater obedience from me, why have you made me as I am? Why have you set me in opposition to yourself? Why not cleanse me of my innate weaknesses and my sins? At this point Pina e Mello breaks off. He is mad, he says, to question the divine wisdom, and he turns to a passionate and humble prayer to God Almighty for mercy, and then to the Virgin. It is the Virgin who will intercede for the Portuguese and plead their case before God; it is Our Lady alone who can turn away the divine wrath.

In the context of this whole discourse, as in the context of the whole poem, Pina e Mello's grievance against God is mildly put and quickly hidden away in the soothing assurances that he knows should be made. But that the earthquake should so profoundly affect him that he had to say these things is for eighteenth-century Portugal a startling indication of the depth of his feelings. Here was a poet, devotedly orthodox in his faith, hating heresy, with a mind fully made up about sin and consequential divine punishment, scorning science and absolutely refusing to believe that the earth moved round the sun, who was so shocked by the Lisbon earthquake that within a few days of its happening he had asked aloud if God was just.

The publication of the *Parénesis* created a flattering stir in the small literary circle of Pina e Mello's contemporary Portuguese writers, but the discussion was for the most part confined to a captious squabble about its form. A writer using the name Sigismundo António Coutinho, who disliked the modern French style, attacked the poem at once, writing from the Arrabida district near Setúbal to which he had fled after the earthquake and where (he says) he was busily repenting under religious guidance his former frivolous life in Lisbon. He said he was unfitted to criticize the work of so great and so learned a poet as Pina e Mello, who had already collected for himself a most useful claque of admirers; but he had to admit he found the poem lacking in taste and poor in composition. It did not even start right, for the poet ought not to have given a poem in Portuguese a Latin (*sic*) title. And he should not have written in verse at all, a most unsuitable vehicle in which to say proper things about such a tragic event as an earthquake; verse is soothing soft stuff, and one required here either rugged oratory or a calm factual prose. Ambassadors and ministers do not conduct their business in verse, said Coutinho, piling all the scorn of the "ancients" on this example of modernity. In the very first page there is a mistranslation of Ecclesiastes i. 4; the poet uses the verb *descender* incorrectly and introduces non-Portuguese words; he is guilty of pleonasm (for example, *bárbara ignorância*) and a shameless prosopopeia in pretending that the earth talks through earthquake-cracks; and there is a passage in which Pina e Mello writes of a city as a world market without making it plain to this critic whether he meant Lisbon or Bahia in Brazil; he says there is now no more left of it than a miserable memory. If he refers to Bahia, how does he know it has been destroyed utterly? If he is really talking about Lisbon, everyone knows he is exaggerating, and when he talks of Neptune raising his sceptre over the emporium—who gave Neptune authority to raise his sceptre on land? What a lot of errors in five lines!

The *Parénesis* seemed to be a very silly poem to those who did not believe that the earthquake was the action of a suddenly furious God, deliberately and indiscriminately wreaking His frightful vengeance on a sinful city. Another poem, written by António da Silva Figueiredo in advocacy of the theory of natural causes, quotes the passage in which Pina e Mello describes how the earthquake strikes alike at high and low, rich and poor, levelling all men to the common status of a miserable victim; for in Silva Figueiredo's view it is precisely this cruelly unjust mass-slaughtering of good and bad alike that shows God is *not* the immediate cause of the earthquake, even though an earthquake has its origin in a natural order that God Himself had permitted to be earthquake-producing. This argument against Pina e Mello is simply that God would have been an unjust God *if* He had deliberately wrecked Lisbon, and Silva Figueiredo does not take advantage of the pessimism and doubt that are expressed in the *Parénesis;* to discover this mood again, more strongly and strangely presented, in these minor Portuguese writings of the time we must turn to a pamphlet written in 1756 and published in 1757 by João Chrisostomo de Faria Cordeiro de Vasconcellos de Sá, known as the author of a little collection of congratulatory verses addressed to King José that had appeared five years previously. The intention of this *Defensam Apologetica* was to defend Pina e Mello against the attack of the writer who called himself Coutinho, which was easy enough since this author had nothing but silly quibbles to offer as objections; but having dealt with these, Faria Cordeiro took the opportunity of printing a poem of his own, apparently with the idea that his readers might see by comparison between this and the *Parénesis* what a good poem that was. It is an eclogue written before he had seen the *Parénesis*. The story it tells is this:

Menalio and Aonio, two shepherds, are about to attend a village feast, but Aonio is in a depressed mood, for he finds life very hard and he is gloomily preoccupied with thoughts about the folly of careless optimism and the overshadowing terror of God's frequently provoked anger. Before the feast and the arrival of their friend Frondoso from the city, they go into the village church, and while they are there an earthquake takes place, damaging the church and killing many people who were inside it. The two shepherds escape, and find that the whole countryside has suffered severely; as the tremors cease Aonio exclaims that though God has temporarily suspended the punishment He is inflicting on the people for sins they have committed, the two shepherds are obviously still in danger. They then come upon the wrecked preparations for the feast, and now Menalio agrees sadly that a world in which joy can be so quickly reduced to sorrow and fright is indeed an appalling place. Everything in life is uncertain, replies Aonio, and while they are reflecting that God has at least spared their lives Frondoso arrives in a state of great alarm and distress.

Frondoso had been in the town during the earthquake and he has come to describe the appalling destruction and the horrors he witnessed among the ruins of its buildings and streets. Aonio says he must at any rate thank God for his escape from death, inasmuch as the disaster, even though naturally caused, is a manifestation of the Eternal Power. He then speaks of the damage and loss of life that the earthquake has caused in the country and describes the dangers he and Menalio have escaped, for instance a rock crashing down from the mountain that nearly killed him. The great mistake he and his friends have made, he says, is that of being optimistic and forgetting the real lot of mankind. Life is not an opportunity for personal advancement. It is a brief dream to be endured without protest. Ambition and discontent are fatal, and we run a continual risk of being punished by Heaven if we do not meekly accept our appointed destinies. It is indeed true that pride goes before a fall. The only thing to do now is for all three of them to stay where they are, accepting in full submission to divine Providence the terrible warning they have had. Frondoso is glad to take this advice and to remain in the hills, for he thinks that country folk have a better idea of their station in life than the townsmen. Menalio agrees; at any single moment the joyful assurance of the thoughtless man may be turned into bitter anguish. And then Aonio concludes that to avoid such tragedy we must set aside all thought of riches and advancement. He who is a shepherd, let him contentedly remain a shepherd, and let lords look after their own dignities and power; but for us, let it suffice that we are content to look after our sheep and lead a quiet village life.

> Pois só e para nós bastante idéa
> Guardar ovelhas, e viver na aldéa.

It is not a forced compliment to Faria Cordeiro that after describing his poem we should now turn at once to Voltaire. Faria Cordeiro felt about the earthquake what Voltaire felt; indeed, had Candide taken part in the dismal discussion between Aonio, Menalio, and Frondoso he might have suitably interjected at almost any point the celebrated remark with which he concludes the novel in which he appears. The shepherds substituted looking after their sheep for Candide's cultivation of his garden; but they all four thought alike; in such a dangerous world attempt nothing but one's simple and immediate way of earning one's living. It is certainly notable that in the context of this heavily censored and unpretentious Portuguese literature Faria Cordeiro should have given unambiguous expression to that variety of pessimism which found its most famous utterance in Voltaire's novel and in his *Poème sur le désastre de Lisbonne*. Pina e Mello had momentarily given way to the impatience of Job; but he had himself brushed aside as impious his outcry against the injustice of God; Faria Cordeiro allowed no softening of his shepherds' grievances; the earthquake had taught them they lived in a cruel world. After the earthquake they were not going to admit that everything that happens happens for the best, that whatever is, is right.

Chapter Seven

OPTIMISM ATTACKED

Now we pass from Portuguese to French literature,[1] to Voltaire and to Rousseau, beginning at once with Voltaire's poem on the Lisbon earthquake, which he wrote very soon after hearing the news of the disaster.[2] In his preface to it he says that its purpose was to expose the folly of the popular optimism derived from Pope's *Essay on Man* (1733-34), an optimism that he calls the *tout est bien* philosophy. If, he asks, when Lisbon, Mequinez, Tetuán, and so many other towns were destroyed with multitudes of their inhabitants in November 1755, the philosophers had said to the wretched survivors, "Whatever happens is for the best; the heirs of the dead will benefit financially; the building-trade will enjoy a

[1] On the subject of French thought concerning the Lisbon earthquake see B. Rohrer, *Das Erdbeben von Lissabon in der französischen Literatur des achtzehnten Jahrhunderts*, Heidelberg, 1933; also W. H. Barber, *Leibniz in France: from Arnauld to Voltaire*, Oxford, 1955. I am sorry I did not read this important book before I wrote the chapter that follows. I am, however, indebted to Mr. Theodore Besterman's *Voltaire et le désastre de Lisbonne: ou la mort de l'Optisme*, which the author was kind enough to show me in advance of its delivery and publication in the *Travaux* of the Institut et Musée Voltaire.

[2] The main idea expressed in the poem was in his mind by 24 November 1755; cf. his letter to Robert Tronchin of that date. *Lettres inédites aux Tronchin*, I, CIX. Geneva, 1950. The first version of the poem had been written by 7 December.

boom; animals will grow fat on meals provided by the corpses trapped in the debris; an earthquake is a necessary effect of a necessary cause; private misfortune must not be overrated; an individual who is unlucky is contributing to the general good"—would not such a speech be as cruel as the earthquake itself was destructive? We cannot turn our backs on the suffering this calamity has caused and pretend it is all some kind of benefit in disguise. We must admit there is evil, positive and inexcusable evil, in the world, and *that* in short, said Voltaire, was the message of his poem. Let men henceforth think of ruined Lisbon and stop deluding themselves with the silly cliché *tout est bien;* the truth is otherwise. *Le mal est sur la terre.*

Today we wonder that it should ever have been necessary to conduct such an argument, but when Voltaire wrote his poem the popular philosophy of optimism, the *tout est bien* kind to which he referred, had forgotten, or rather had chosen to ignore, the formidable significance of the problem presented to man by the existence of moral and physical evil. Evil was something that could be left in the background, unattended, a disagreeable and grating, but all the same necessary, part of the machinery that worked the world. This kind of optimism was not a variety of thought confined to readers of the learned periodicals, to scholars acquainted with Leibniz's *Théodicée* and *Monadologie,* and to the intelligentsia who discussed Pope's *Essay on Man;* it was a force generally inspiring a contentment with the world as men then found it, a universal mood that had become, as Professor Basil Willey has said, "in essence an apologia for the status quo." [3] It was not even mainly an aristocratic mood, a kind of extravagant Versailles carelessness, but a popular creed. Almost every generalization about eighteenth-century thought can be strongly contradicted, but there is good reason for saying that most men at the time of the Lisbon earthquake were comfortably sure that the world was a good place in which everything that happened was on a long view likely to be "for the best," and so they lived their lives as happily as they could, very little troubled by any responsibility for the alleviation of collective unhappiness.

It is true enough that Voltaire first of all attacked this optimism in the form in which he found it in Pope's poem, for the famous passage at the end of the First Epistle beginning "Cease then, nor ORDER Imperfection name," condensed into a conspicuous bull's-eye precisely the sentiments to which he objected; and later he made Leibniz the butt of his novel *Candide*. But he was not conducting an academic argument, and it is certainly true that the Lisbon earthquake-controversy in France did not depend upon a thorough re-examination of the theodicy of Gottfried Wilhelm Leibniz (1646-1716), which was imperfectly understood in that country and disliked by the Church as fatalistic. Voltaire really did not know much about what Leibniz had actually said, but with some justification he took the clichés of the Leibnizian theodicy as symptomatic of popular optimism and poured upon them in *Candide* his own brilliant variety of destructive scorn. [4]

[3] *The Eighteenth Century Background*, p. 48. London, 1953. On this subject cf. pp. 41-42 *ante*.

[4] Leibniz said that God, perfect in love, wisdom, and power, after considering all the logically possible worlds, created the world in which

The importance of Voltaire's part in the moralizing over the Lisbon earthquake is that he had something to say to which a large audience would pay attention; for he was addressing contemporary European society on a general matter of conscience, knowing that the news of the earthquake was likely to have made his hearers in an unexpected measure vulnerable. Long before the earthquake took place, he had himself lost faith in this general optimism, and he felt that this calamity provided an incontestable and grisly proof that he was right in rejecting the *tout est bien* doctrine. He believed that everyone would now have to admit that man dare not hope for a safe life in this world under the benevolent protection

there was the greatest excess of good over evil. God had therefore decided that a world containing no evil would not have been so good a world as this world, which does contain evil. Once this world was created and evil of various kinds admitted into it, God cannot logically intervene to prevent evil from fulfilling its appointed role, because to do this would imply that God had not chosen the best possible world. The theory of the pre-established harmony, which is the subject of much jesting in *Candide*, is a consequence of the theory of the monads which had forced Leibniz to the conclusion that at the time of the creation once and for all God had ordered everything that was ever going to happen (*Theodicy* 9). Therefore, we can be sure that a world in which there were no such things as disastrous earthquakes would not be so good a world as one in which they do occur. Leibniz, however, did not rate earthquakes very high as evil things. "One Caligula alone, one Nero, has caused more evil than an earthquake," he said (*Theodicy* 26). What we have to remember is that if we could understand the universal harmony, we should see that what we describe as a completely evil thing is a proper part of the plan most worthy of being chosen; in a word, we should ourselves understand that what God has done is the best (*Dissertation* 44). Leibniz, however, would not have said that the Lisbon earthquake was a disguised blessing, for he admitted that what was "best" in the infinite wisdom of God may seem to us to be only a painful and wasteful act of destruction, however much we may try to see some good in it; nor would he have said that the earthquake was a suddenly contrived punishment of the Lisbon people. Yet we *are* led to grace by the ways of nature (*Monadology* 88), and the mechanism of the physical world, determined at the creation, works in harmony with the course of its moral government, also determined at the creation.

of a Providence that could be counted on to reward virtuous behaviour. Man was weak and helpless, ignorant of his destiny, and exposed to terrible dangers, as all must now see; the optimism of the age must be replaced by something that is not much more than an apprehensive hope that Providence will lead us through our dangerous world to a happier state. *Un jour tout sera bien* should be the new limit of optimistic thought.

Later, commenting on the Lisbon earthquake, Voltaire said that its effect was to make men introspective, by which he meant apprehensive about their mortality and ultimate destiny, and that wise observation should always be the first answer to the question—in what way did the Lisbon earthquake influence European thought? Dreadful doubts and fears chilled the hearts of men when they considered what the Lisbon earthquake must really have been like to those who died in it and to those who lived through it. No doubt, in their full intensity these doubts and fears were short-lived, and in many cases of the most superficial kind; but Voltaire knew that, and he regretted the way in which the world turned quickly again to its pleasures, trying to forget the earthquake as soon as possible, in the excitements of dancing, the theatre, and the lottery. Yet the tremendous shock that the news had caused could not be completely absorbed by such feeble defences. Men were frightened. They asked what really was the part they had to play in God's scheme for the universe; what really was the nature of the Providence under whose protection they thought they lived; what, in fact, was their relation to God?

The *Poème sur le désastre de Lisbonne* is addressed directly to men in this mood, and, once in circulation, it was widely read and discussed, for it was the comment of one of the wisest men in Europe on a disaster that had shocked Western civilization more than any other event since the fall of Rome in the fifth century. As the poem was written so soon after the earthquake, Voltaire inevitably made some use of the earliest reports about the calamity; but he did not need gruesome overstatements to make the effect he wanted, and he knew quite well that the first accounts of the earthquake that reached Switzerland would need revision. "It is said that half the town is still standing," he wrote on 16 December. "There is a tendency to exaggerate both good tidings and bad tidings on their first announcement." [5] His poem obtained its hearing, because it dealt directly with the perplexity filling the minds of his readers, and because it is movingly inspired by sorrow for the people of Lisbon. Condorcet, his biographer, said that though Voltaire was over sixty when he wrote this poem, his soul, deeply stirred by the suffering of humanity, had all the zest and all the fire of youth. Voltaire's melancholy is indeed strongly expressed, and it is all the more powerful a force because he has so little comfort to offer humanity in place of the brittle optimism he was now determined to destroy.

The poem is addressed to the deluded *philosophes* who tell everybody that all is for the best. They are told to look at tragic shattered Lisbon and its smoking ruins, and to think of the excruciating fate of the hundred thousand victims of the earthquake. Hearing their cries, seeing them being burnt alive or suffering other unspeakable tortures, are the philosophers going to tell us that all this

---

[5] Voltaire gives a revised reference to the Lisbon earthquake in the *Précis du siècle de Louis XV* (Moland), xv, 335-36.

is part of the good providence of a benevolent God? Are we going to be told of these pitiful heaps of corpses that they are the bodies of sinners who are justly the victims of God's anger because of their crimes?

> Quel crime, quelle faute ont commis ces enfants
> Sur le sein maternel écrasés et sanglants?
> Lisbonne, qui n'est plus, eut-elle plus de vices
> Que Londres, que Paris, plongés dans les délices?
> Lisbonne est abîmée, et l'on danse a Paris.

The fine philosophers, comfortably far away from all this suffering, would talk very differently if such a disaster had befallen their own towns; then we should hear them crying out at the horrors that had afflicted them, and then they would recognize that a great earthquake brings nothing but miserable evil on man. *Le bien fut pour Dieu seul.*[6]

> Croyez-moi, quand la terre entr'ouvre ses abîmes,
> Ma plainte est innocente et mes cris légitimes.

Are you going to tell me that pride is deceiving me, that pride makes me rebel against suffering?

> Allez interroger les rivages du Tage;
> Fouillez dans les débris de ce sanglant ravage;
> Demandez aux mourants, dans ce séjour d'effroi,
> Si c'est l'orgueil qui crie: "O Dieu, secourez-moi! [7]
> O Ciel, ayez pitié de l'humaine misère!"

We are told that all is for the best and that everything that happens must happen, but would the universe really be a worse place if it had not been found necessary to

[6] From a variant passage in a Geneva edition of 1756.
[7] In the final version, "O Ciel, secourez-moi."

destroy Lisbon? Could not an omniscient and omnipotent God achieve His purpose otherwise? If there must be earthquakes why could not the ghastly things happen in the middle of the desert?

Je respecte mon Dieu, mais j'aime l'univers.

Will the wretched victims die consoled when you tell them that the earthquake happened for the general good? that Lisbon will be rebuilt? that it will become populous again? that northern Europe will become rich as a result of their losses? that all evil things that happen to us are according to the "general law" good things? that these poor people in their death-agonies and the worms that are about to devour them are alike playing their proper part in God's master plan? What horrible talk!

Voltaire will have nothing more to do with the dreadful doctrine of unchangeable laws of necessity. He believes God is free, just, and merciful, so why do we have to suffer as we do? It is all very well to launch the furies of Heaven against rocks and trees; they do not feel. But man is alive and sensitive. He cannot help crying out in his misery. A pot, liable to be broken, does not ask the potter why it was made such a poor, coarse, brittle thing; for the potter did not give it a heart or feeling. Man will not be satisfied by being told that his misfortune is for somebody else's good.

De mon corps tout sanglant mille insectes vont naître;
Quand la mort met le comble aux maux que j'ai soufferts,
Le beau soulagement d'être mangé des vers!

It is easy to say that one suffering man is negligible in relation to God's whole design for the universe, but all living creatures seem to be condemned to existence in a ferocious world of pain and mutual slaughter. How can anyone say with conviction *tout est bien?* The world around us denies it, and the secret terrors of the philosophers must have told them a hundred times that it is not true.

> Elements, animaux, humains, tout est en guerre,
> Il le faut avouer, le *mal* est sur la terre:

And where has this evil come from? Can it possibly proceed from the Author of all good things? One cannot stomach the idea that a benevolent God, loving His people and prodigally bestowing His benefits upon them, at the same time pours down every possible misfortune on their wretched heads. We listen to all the confusing and contradictory theodicies, and while we are arguing Lisbon crashes into smoking dust, and the shock of a great earthquake shatters towns all the way from the Tagus to Cádiz.

Voltaire shows that no theory resting on optimism and a belief in a kind and loving God can explain why mankind should have been afflicted with such sorrow and suffering as the earthquake caused. He turns upon Leibniz. How does he explain the presence of all this misery in his "best of all possible worlds"? How does he account for the fact that the innocent suffer equally with the guilty? And now the poem moves to its terrible conclusion. We know nothing; nature has no message for us; God does not speak:

> On a besoin d'un Dieu qui parle au genre humain.
> Il n'appartient qu'à lui d'expliquer son ouvrage,
> De consoler le faible, et d'éclairer le sage.

Men are weak, grovelling, ignorant creatures, their bodies made for decay and their minds for grief. They know nothing of their origin or purpose or destiny:

Atomes tourmentés sur cet amas de boue,
Que la mort engloutit, et dont le sort se joue,
Mais atomes pensants, atomes dont les yeux,
Guidés par la pensée, ont mesuré les cieux;
Au sein de l'infini, nous élançons notre être,
Sans pouvoir un moment nous voir et nous connaître.
Que faut-il, o Mortels! Mortels, il faut souffrir,
Se soumettre en silence, adorer, et mourir.

Before it was printed Voltaire was curious to know what the effect of his poem would be when it was read in hostile or suspicious or easily offended religious circles. Of the first draft he had suggested in a lighthearted letter of 19 December 1755 to his most trusted old friend the Comte d'Argental that these verses were really only suitable for private circulation among the *philosophes;* [8] he did not want to be thought *mauvais théologien,* and he was prepared to take some trouble to alter his poem so that it should not offend the heresy-hunters or the timid thinkers. Later on, in April 1756, he wrote of this poem and of the deistic *La Loi Naturelle,* published with it, to another very old friend, Cideville, "I had to make my way of thinking clear; it is not that either of a superstitious person or of an atheist. I am inclined to think that respectable folk will share my view." With the Lisbon earthquake-poem, the main trouble was the ending. Bertrand, the pastor of the French Church at Berne (*see* p.

---

[8] MS. Louis Clarke. ". . . ils (ces vers tragiques) pourront exercer votre philosofie, et cette de votre Société. Je les crois aussi sages quel est possible, et de nature cependant a n'etre qu'en vos mains."

167), had told him that the pessimism of the last lines was hurtful and too violently expressed. Voltaire met the objections by introducing "to hope" in the concluding line:

> Mortels, il faut souffrir,
> Se soumettre, adorer, espérer, et mourir.

That was in February 1756, and his friends did not think it adequate; so, as he did not want his "sermon" to shock orthodox theologians too violently, he composed a new ending to it about the time the first printed edition of the original version appeared in Geneva, that is, in March 1756. In this second and, so to speak, definitive version of the *Poème sur le désastre de Lisbonne* the last two lines are omitted, and the poem is continued with the observation that there is a great and often painful chase after happiness in progress in this world; we can at least say we are sometimes able temporarily to forget our sorrows, and there is always the blessing of being able to hope.

> *Un jour tout sera bien,* voilà notre espérance,
> *Tout est bien aujourd'hui,* voilà l'illusion.
> Les sages me trompaient, et Dieu seul a raison.

I shall not blame Providence, said Voltaire. I myself used to write in a light, happy vein, but:

> D'autres temps, d'autres moeurs: instruit par la vieillesse,
> Des humains égarés partageant la faiblesse,
> Dans une épaisse nuit cherchant à m'éclairer,
> Je ne sais que souffrir, et non pas murmurer.

Once upon a time a caliph, dying, addressed this prayer to the God he worshipped:

"Je t'apporte, ô seul roi, seul être illimité,
Tout ce que tu n'as pas dans ton immensité,
Les défauts, les regrets, les maux, et l'ignorance,"
Mais il pouvait encore ajouter *l'espérance*.

There exists a copy corrected in Voltaire's hand that turns the last line into a question, as if Voltaire felt that his concessions to orthodox thought had gone a little too far.[9]

The early history of the poem and its first effects on French readers can be illustrated by reference to one or two other poems on the earthquake of about the same date. In the first place, almost anything might be expected of Voltaire, and in fact the circulation of his poem in Paris was preceded there by the appearance of some verses, believed to be by him, which were really written by his young friend the Marquis de Ximenez, an outspoken free-thinker whose poem caused much offence. Ximenez was not prepared to say with Voltaire, *Je respecte mon Dieu*, and his main point was that the much-advertised piety of the Portuguese had proved useless as a protection against an implacable and inexplicable God who had suddenly determined to obliterate Lisbon. He asked of what use were the armies of monks, the bloody labours of the Inquisition, the stores of relics, and the endless offerings made to thousands of saints? They were all now proved to be worthless as a means of propitiating God. Heretic England was now laughing at the devotions of the Roman Church. The pirates of Algiers could now plunder Portugal happily; Heaven was on *their* side.

[9] Mais pouvait-il encore ajouter l'espérance? See George R. Havens: *Modern Language Notes*, XLIV (1929), pp. 489 ff.

O Providence, if sometimes in despair we lose faith in you:

> C'est quand le bras qui frappe la vertu,
> N'a pas au moins commencé par le crime.

One of the consequences of the great earthquake that had caused much distress in French literary society was the death of the young Racine, son of the poet Louis Racine, and grandson of Jean Racine, the dramatist. This unfortunate youth was drowned in the seismic wave that poured over the slender isthmus between the city of Cádiz and the mainland, with the result that his wretched father, brokenhearted, went into complete retirement. Several poets attempted to console him with offerings of verse, and one of these pieces, by Jean Jacques Lefranc, Marquis de Pompignan, was published in the *Journal Encyclopédique* next to the poem of the impious Marquis de Ximenez as a wholesome corrective. This presents us with the opposite point of view, the complacent attitude to disaster that Voltaire wished to disturb and shame.

In fifteen verses this simple, serious man, who so hated the *philosophes* that he described their work in this poem as *recherches pleines d'imposture* and *essais pusillanimes*, who, after his inaugural address to the Académie Français in 1760 was so ridiculed, chiefly by Voltaire, that he was forced into retirement, this godly man summarized ineptly but with Christian bluntness the pious resignation that most of all irritated his opponents. Young Racine is at peace in Heaven. We on earth grieve, but at the same time we know that the innocent are required to suffer while in this world, and we do not complain, because

Christians are sure that the sufferers will be recompensed in their future life. Presumptuous *philosophes* who depend on scientific explanations of calamities like the Lisbon earthquake have no such consolation; they try to shut God out of their minds and to forget that an earthquake may be the result of His anger. We, on the other hand, have our faith, a faith that can overcome the very worst griefs. Let us expect nothing as certain in this life but the inevitable hour of death, death that is to be followed by eternal happiness or eternal damnation.

Voltaire's *Poème sur le désastre de Lisbonne* was printed in a censored form in the *Journal Encyclopédique* for April 1756, with an introductory note explaining that since the flame of his genius sometimes led him to stray beyond the limits that a good Christian ought to observe, a few short passages likely to cause offence had been omitted, their place being marked by asterisks. Immediately after this comes a *Réponse à Mr. De V. . . . ou Défense de l'Axiome, Tout est bien,* a poem by an anonymous author who thought that, though one may grieve over the fate of Lisbon, it was blasphemous presumption to question God's goodness because of the earthquake, thus condemning as an evil thing an event that God Himself had decided should take place. A slave has no right to question a slave-master. God commands, and man must obey in total submission, receiving the gifts of Providence with gratitude and divine punishment in meek and unprotesting shame. One of these gifts is hope. Even the earthquake-victim's pitiful cry, "O God, help me," expresses a hope that mercifully lessens the agony of death in an earthquake. The truth is that we fear death too much, said this poet, in company with other writers who were shocked by Voltaire's pessimism.

We come to the heart of the controversy with Rousseau's letter to Voltaire of 18 August 1756.[10] Rousseau was then forty-three, known as a musician and as the author of a famous essay, *Discours sur les arts et sciences,* in which he had delighted civilized France by proving the superiority of the savage state; but his most celebrated works had not yet been published. He had no open quarrel with Voltaire, who had arranged for the little volume containing *La Loi Naturelle* and the poem on the earthquake to be sent to him; probably Rousseau was already envious of Voltaire's fame and had smarted under his witty criticism of the *Discours;* but the letter is not a display of polemical fireworks set off merely to irritate the great man; on the contrary, it is a sincere expression of something Rousseau felt he had got to say, and he began by saying that he entirely approved of *La Loi Naturelle.* It was the earthquake poem that had upset him.

Rousseau rejected Voltaire's gloomy picture of man's unhappy fate on earth. He said that the optimism attacked in the poem had helped him to endure the very things supposed to be unendurable. Man must be patient, recognizing evil as a necessary consequence of his own nature and of the nature of the universe. A benevolent God desired to preserve man from evil, and of all the possible systems whereby His creation might be ordered, He had chosen the one that contained the least evil and the most good. Put bluntly, said Rousseau, the reason why God had not done better for mankind was that He could

[10] *Lettre de J. J. Rousseau citoyen de Genève à Monsieur de Voltaire.* First published 1759.

not do better. Voltaire, on the other hand, argues that an omnipotent God could have prevented evil from tarnishing His creation, and the fact that He did not do so means that the only discoverable reason for our existence on earth is that we are here in order to suffer and to die. That view Rousseau could not accept. He maintained that moral evil originated in man himself, and that, even though physical evil is a necessary part of the creation, the majority of physical evils are man's own fault. This did not dispose of Voltaire's argument; indeed, Voltaire agreed that man was responsible for much of the evil in the world; [11] but Rousseau wanted to put the case in its most extreme form.

Consider Lisbon, for example. It was not nature that had congregated twenty thousand houses of six or seven stories on that particular site. If the inhabitants of the city had not chosen to crowd themselves together in dangerous buildings, the damage would have been much less. Had they dwelt properly distributed and in smaller houses they could have escaped easily at the first shock and have been far from the danger-centre by the next day; but they stayed obstinately on the spot, worrying about their money and their possessions, and many were killed in consequence.

Everyone would agree with Voltaire in wishing the earthquake had taken place in the middle of a desert rather than at Lisbon. There *are* earthquakes in deserts, but we do not hear much about them as they do no harm

[11] In a letter to Pastor Allamand of Bex of 16 December 1755, referring to the Lisbon earthquake, Voltaire said, "Je plains comme vous les portugais; mais les hommes se font encore plus de mal sur leur petite taupinière que ne leur en fait la nature. Nos guerres égorgent plus d'hommes que les tremblements de terre n'en engloutissent."

to the precious town-dwellers, and merely frighten a few savages who are sensible enough to live scattered over a large area and do not have to fear falling roofs and burning houses. What does Voltaire really mean? Are the town-dwellers' requirements to alter the laws of nature? Man cannot talk in this way. We cannot so arrange matters that to prevent an earthquake at a certain place, we have only got to go and set up a town there!

Rousseau's general case in favour of the *tout est bien* school of thought depends on the usual arguments. It is not always a misfortune to be killed suddenly. Providence is a universal supervision of God's creation and is not concerned with what happens to an individual creature during his brief appearance on earth. And so on. The important part of the letter is Rousseau's perception of the fundamental difference between the kind of man who is a pessimist, and the kind of man who is an optimist, in regard to the circumstances of our mortal life. Voltaire is accused of thinking that few people would wish to be reborn to live again the same kind of life they have already lived. He got that idea from Erasmus, said Rousseau, and he went on to ask whom Voltaire had actually consulted on this point? Bored, stupid, frightened rich people? Or his fellow-writers, a sedentary, unhealthy, unhappy lot of men? He ought to have consulted an honest *bourgeois*, a good craftsman, or one of his Swiss peasants. Rousseau said there was probably not one single highlander of the "haut Valais" who was tired of his simple existence and would not exchange Paradise for the chance to be reborn time after time so that he could go on living his accustomed uneventful life for ever and ever.

In a famous passage at the end of the letter Rousseau

presents the problem as the personal difference between himself and Voltaire:

> Je ne puis m'empêcher, Monsieur, de remarquer à ce propos une opposition bien singulière entre vous et moi dans le sujet de cette lettre. Rassasié de gloire et désabusé des vaines grandeurs vous viviez libre au sein de l'abondance, bien sûr de l'immortalité vous philosophez paisiblement sur la nature de l'ame, et si le corps ou le coeur souffre vous avez Tronchain pour Médecin et pour Ami; vous ne trouvez pourtant que mal sur la terre; et moi, homme obscur, pauvre, et tourmenté d'un mal sans remède, je médite avec plaisir dans ma retraite, et je trouve que tout est bien.

And how is this difference to be explained? The answer is to be found in the word *hope* with which Voltaire ended his poem. His variety of hope is vague and dubious, and without anything better than that, worldly happiness and prosperity, such as he enjoys, is worth nothing; therefore he is a pessimist. But Rousseau possesses hope of another kind, strong and certain, a hope that illumines and beautifies everything in his life. He can tolerate no doubt on the subject of the immortality of the soul and the heavenly recompense that he will receive for his suffering on earth. God is kind. *Tout est bien.* Rousseau was absolutely sure.

We see now that the arguments about God's providence that were the result of the Lisbon earthquake are in detail not very important. As Rousseau had said earlier in this same letter, for the pious Providence is always right and for the *philosophes* it is always wrong. Men have a conviction one way or the other, and this conviction cannot be altered for one party by pointing to the unjust death of innocent people, or for the other party by observing that premature death saves its victims from a gruesome death-bed agony in old age and sends them to Heaven unembarrassed by a load of sins that they would have committed had they lived. Therefore, we need not examine in full the small pros and cons of this unavailing dispute; but we cannot leave the matter without noting one or two more expressions of opinion. And, finally, there is *Candide*.

First there is Immanuel Kant, aged thirty-one, at the beginning of his great career and still closely adhering to the optimistic philosophy of Leibniz. When the news of the Lisbon earthquake reached Königsberg the townsfolk, as was generally the case in Germany, were exceedingly alarmed and also full of sympathy for the Portuguese; but young Kant seems to have been first of all more interested in the event as a scientific problem than as a tragedy that had destroyed a city and led to great loss of life. He published three short papers on the subject in 1756, reviewing theories of the causes of earthquakes and recording all the attendant phenomena of the 1755 shock, the widespread nature of which had strongly impressed him. He even includes a note on the beneficial aspect of earthquakes. Just as we complain of ill-timed or excessive rain, forgetting that rain feeds the springs necessary in our economy, so we denounce earthquakes, refusing to consider whether they, too, may not bring us good things. Are they, in the first place, really as bad as we make out? We lament the dead; but all men must die. We grieve over the loss of property; but property is not everlasting.

Our cities of high houses will inevitably be destroyed if we build them in places like Lisbon. Earthquakes are a part of nature; and instead of expecting nature to suit our convenience we must accommodate ourselves to nature. On the credit side let us remember that the subterranean fire that is the cause of earthquakes also gives us hot springs and baths; it has also formed the valuable mineral ores in the rocks; vegetation benefits by the release of subterranean substances; the escaping sulphur fumes have a welcome sanitary effect. It is possible the world itself would not really be a warm enough place to support life properly without this subterranean fire. It may occasionally do great damage, but it seems very likely that we could not get on without it, and we ought to be grateful for it.

Finally, Kant added a short note about earthquakes in relation to God's government of the world. In this, his pre-critical and Leibnizian period, he could offer only small comfort, pointing out that at least we are not the helpless victims of a dangerous natural order that may irresponsibly destroy us at any time, because the course of our lives in prosperity and adversity has been determined by God. However, his modest postscript is historically interesting. In his later life he rejected any theodicy dependent on our reasoning about God's purpose, since he maintained that human reason was powerless in this respect, and even in this early footnote to a natural history paper he condemned the interpretation of the Lisbon earthquake as the punishment of a sinful town, not because such an interpretation was uncharitable, but because it was a shocking act of impertinence to offer any opinion at all on such a subject. We cannot possibly know why God allowed this earthquake to happen. We must remember that man is not the only object of divine care; God in His inscrutable wisdom presides over the whole gigantic content of nature, and it may be necessary that the ordering of the universe should include events unfavourable to man. But at this point Kant makes an important observation. In practice, he says, we are not left in any uncertainty. We know what we must think and what we must do. We know that this disaster teaches us that we were not created for life in the present world only and that we cannot expect our longing for happiness to be fully satisfied here; we know also that it is now more than ever our business to love our neighbours and do all that we can to make this world a pleasant place. This is the germ of Kant's subsequent view that the only possible theodicy is a practical act of faith in divine justice. If our reason can assure us that there is a God, and that He is good, then our lives must be lived in absolute loyalty to Him, however grievous the misfortunes of ourselves or our fellow-men.

Another young man who wrote on this subject was Louis de Beausobre (1730-83), son of a Protestant theologian who had taken refuge in Berlin and won the favour of Frederick the Great. He had been sent to Paris for his education, and there he wrote a book called *Essai sur le Bonheur,* which was published in 1758. In this he fought a fine battle on behalf of the *tout est bien* school of thought. He said there was far too much crying out about the horrors of a great disaster like the Lisbon earthquake; in fact, he thought the *frivoles déclamateurs,* wailing about the tragedy in Portugal, were probably not so grieved as they pretended to be, and that there was a

great deal of exaggeration and insincerity. Men forget the
blessings and happiness of normal life when they are suddenly shocked by a great disaster; they think only of grief
and suffering, and say God's providence has failed them.
What does it all amount to? asked Louis de Beausobre.
The earthquake victims are dead; but death is not a
greater evil when it strikes many people simultaneously
than when it removes them one by one at intervals, so
why should death suddenly be deemed so awful when it
is accompanied by the quaking of the earth? Why is it
specially sad to die in a disaster? And what is so terrible
about a disaster like this earthquake? A lot of riches are
lost; but man can get on without them. Overthrown cities
can be rebuilt. A great calamity is just a multiplication
of the ordinary calamities that may happen to anyone
without causing any general alarm. Suffering simultaneously with others does not make suffering worse, and all
that can really be said about an earthquake as an evil
thing is that it causes a greater total amount of grief on
one occasion than a single accident. At which we may be
sorry; but, after all, plagues, war, famine, and earthquakes
are divine punishments on mankind, and we cannot expect them to be pleasant.

If this young gentleman was thinking of Voltaire when
he referred to the *frivoles déclamateurs* and believed he
had scored a point or two against the *Poème sur le désastre de Lisbonne,* he was very quickly made aware of
his mistake, for in the following year (1759) *Candide* was
published, and the whole *tout est bien* philosophy was
thereby blown to pieces in company with poor Louis de
Beausobre's book and everything else of the kind to the

accompaniment of the derisive laughter of literary Europe. Voltaire had not changed his mind. He disliked more and more the common version of Leibniz's theodicy now that the earthquake had shown its obvious untenability, and he knew there was confusion of thought on this subject since he himself had been classed as an optimist, having once said that he considered it was proved that there was more good than bad in the world.[12] He now knew that there was much evil, unfair, undeserved, cruel evil, for man in this world, and in the autumn and winter of 1758 the thoughts that had been developing in his mind over many years blossomed suddenly into the brilliant little novel that on publication instantly made every glib optimist look a fool. It is the end of the controversy. "After *Candide,* there was no more to be said; the case was finished, and the case was lost." [13]

Candide is, as we have said, directed against Leibniz rather than Pope, for Pangloss, the philosopher, is a German primed with a complete apparatus of clichés and jargon derived from Leibniz's *Théodicée;* but the general target of all this rapid-fire raillery is the uncritical popular mixture of his optimism and Pope's, and the inadequacy of providential protection.[14] The novel is so sim-

---

[12] Cf. Vicomte d'Alès de Corbet, P.A. *De l'origine du Mal,* p. 50. Paris, 1758.

[13] Paul Hazard: *European Thought in the Eighteenth Century,* trans. J. Lewis May, p. 322. London, 1954. Hazard adds, "Not that optimism suddenly disappeared completely; a doctrine lives on for a long time, even when wounded, even when its soul has fled."

[14] David Hume wrote on 12 April 1759 to Adam Smith, "Voltaire has lately published a small work called *Candide ou L'optimisme.* It is full of sprightliness and Impiety, and is indeed a Satyre upon Providence, under Pretext of criticizing the Leibnitian System." *New Letters,* ed. Klibansky and Mossner. Oxford, 1954. William Warburton's judgement on this novel is also interesting: "The real design of *Candide* is to recommend naturalism (i.e. natural religion): the professed design is to

ple in structure that its point could hardly be missed by the most careless reader. Poor Candide, always hankering after the equally unfortunate heroine, Cunégonde, progresses hopefully and trustingly and rapidly through a world packed with every imaginable misery for him, including excruciating physical hardships and cruelly delusive periods of respite. From time to time Dr. Pangloss, who has his own special ration of hardship to endure, appears as his companion and comforter, always ready to justify every new horror befalling the characters in the book as a necessary event in the pre-established harmony of the universe. The story ranges round the world, but early in the tale Candide sails for Lisbon with Pangloss and also the Anabaptist James, who alone had befriended him in Holland. Their ship is caught in a most dreadful storm within sight of Lisbon, and at this point we can have a short extract from the tale itself:

> Half of the passengers, exhausted and violently seasick, were too miserable even to worry about their danger; but the others kept crying out in terror and praying. The sails were torn; the masts broke; the ship began to leak very badly. Those who could tried to keep

ridicule the *optimisme* not of Pope, but of Leibniz, which is founded professedly in fate, and makes a sect in Germany . . . you will wonder perhaps, the translation was made at my recommendation." Warburton-Hurd Letters. 8 July 1759, No. cxxx. It is a tribute to this novel that two English translations, one by William Rider, were published in London in 1759. For the background to *Candide*, see the introduction by André Morize to the edition published by the *Société des textes français modernes*, Paris (Hachette), 1913; also introductions by Richard Aldington in *Candide and other Romances* (Broadway Translations), London, 1927; by H. N. Brailsford in *Candide and Other Tales* (Everyman's Library, No. 936), London, 1937, a volume that contains Smollett's translation revised by James Thornton; by O. R. Taylor in *Candide* (Blackwell's French Texts), Oxford, 1942; and by John Butt to his translation in the Penguin Classics, first published in 1947.

her under control, but nobody knew what ought to be done and nobody gave any orders. The Anabaptist was trying to help on deck when a brutal sailor struck him hard and sent him sprawling, so hard that on the recoil the wretch fell overboard headfirst and hung over the waters hooked up on a bit of broken mast. The kindly Anabaptist picked himself up and tried to rescue him, and he did succeed in hoisting the sailor aboard, but in the effort of doing so he was himself thrown into the sea and was drowned in full view of the man he had saved, who let him perish without even giving him a look. Candide came up at this moment and saw his poor benefactor appear for the last time and then disappear for ever. He wanted to throw himself off into the sea after him, but Pangloss stopped him, pointing out that the Tagus approach to Lisbon had been created on purpose for this Anabaptist to be drowned in it. While he was proving this *a priori*, the ship went down, and every single person lost his life except Pangloss, Candide, and the brutal sailor. This villain swam ashore very comfortably, and eventually Pangloss and Candide also got there on a plank.

When they had recovered a little, they walked towards Lisbon, hoping to get something to eat after their ordeal, as Candide still had some money left; but they had scarcely entered the city when suddenly the earth shook violently under their feet. The sea rose boiling in the harbour and broke up all the craft anchored there; the city burst into flames, and ashes covered the streets and squares; the houses came crashing down, roofs piling up on foundations, and even the foundations were smashed to pieces. Thirty thousand inhabitants of both sexes and all ages were crushed to death under the ruins. The sailor, whistling and swearing,

cried, "We are going to make something out of this!"
Pangloss asked aloud, "Whatever can be the *sufficient
cause* of this phenomenon?" Candide said it must certainly be the Last Day. The sailor, however, plunged
recklessly into the ruins, risked death again and again
to get at money, found some and grabbed it, got drunk,
slept till he was sober, and then got hold of the first
whore he could find among the dead and the dying in
this dreadful pile of ruins. Pangloss tugged him by the
sleeve. "My friend," he said, "this is not right. You have
not properly taken into consideration the *universal reason;* you are timing things badly." "Hell to you," roared
the creature. "I am a sailor, Java-born. I have been
four times to Japan, and have insulted the crucifix each
trip. You've got hold of the wrong man with this universal reason of yours!"

Some falling masonry had hit Candide, and he lay
flat in the street covered with debris. He said to Pangloss, "I am dying. Get me a little wine and oil." "An
earthquake is nothing new," Pangloss replied; "Lima in
America had the same experience last year. Similar
causes, similar effects. Obviously, there is a train of sulphur running under the earth all the way from Lima
to Lisbon." "Nothing is more probable," said Candide;
"but for God's sake get me a little oil and wine." "What
do you mean by probable?" asked Pangloss indignantly.
"I maintain the case is proved." At this point Candide
lost consciousness, and Pangloss brought him some water from a fountain close at hand.

The next day, having found some provisions by
scrambling about among the ruins, they felt a bit better and were able to take part in the relief work. Some
of the survivors in return managed to give them a meal
of a sort, though it was a melancholy affair as every-

body was tearful and depressed, all except Pangloss who comforted them with the assurance that things could not have turned out otherwise than they had done. "For," he said, "all this is necessarily for the best; because if there is a volcano under Lisbon, it could not be anywhere else, since it is impossible that things should not be exactly as they are. For *tout est bien!*"

A little man in black, an officer of the Inquisition, who was sitting beside him, observed politely, "Apparently, Sir, you do not believe in original sin; for if everything is for the best, what becomes of the Fall and punishment for sin?" "I humbly beg Your Excellency's pardon," answered Pangloss, even more politely; "the Fall and the consequent curse upon mankind entered necessarily into the best of possible worlds." "Then you don't believe in free will?" asked the man from the Inquisition. "Your Excellency must excuse me," said Pangloss, "but I assure you free will and absolute necessity are not mutually contradictory terms; for it was necessary that we should be free, because the determinate will . . ." Here he was cut short as the Inquisition official made a sign to his servant who was that moment handing the great philosopher a glass of port.

After the earthquake, which had destroyed three-quarters of Lisbon, the Portuguese pundits could not think of any better way of preventing total ruin than to treat the people to a splendid auto-da-fé, for the University of Coimbra had declared that the spectacle of a number of people being ceremonially burnt over a slow fire was an infallible way of preventing an earthquake. So they seized for this purpose a Basque who had married his godmother, and also two Portuguese caught out in the Jewish trick of refusing to eat the bacon-part of a larded chicken. Pangloss and his pupil Candide were also both arrested at the dinner in the ruins, one for having spoken imprudently, and the other for having listened approvingly. Both of them were marched off and imprisoned separately in extremely cold cells where there was not the slightest danger of their suffering any inconvenience from the sun. A week later they were each dressed up in a *sanbenito* (a heretic's robe) with a paper mitre as a hat. Candide's costume was decorated with flames pointing downwards and devils without tails or claws; but Pangloss's devils had both tails and claws, and his flames were shooting upwards. Thus clothed, they were led off in a procession and listened to a very moving sermon, followed by some nice music in counterpoint. Candide was flogged in rhythm with the chanting; the Basque and the two men who wouldn't eat bacon were burnt, and Pangloss was hanged, though that was not the normal practice at these ceremonies. The same day there was another tremendous and very noisy earthquake that did great damage.

Candide, terrified almost out of his wits, covered with blood, and trembling violently, said to himself, "If this is the best of all possible worlds, whatever must the others be like?"

The sufferers in this novel are a very tough lot. Pangloss, taken down when he was only half dead, recovers consciousness when he is being dissected, and Cunégonde, believed to have been disembowelled by the Bulgars in her ancestral home, turns up in Lisbon having suffered nothing worse than a cut in the groin and frequent raping. At the end of the book, when at last all their trials and disappointments are over, a little party finished up on a small farm near Constantinople. The chief characters assembled are Candide; Cunégonde, now a scraggy old shrew; her ancient attendant, the Pope's daughter, who had a buttock cut off and eaten by Turkish soldiers; Martin, a pessimistic old scholar picked up in America; and Pangloss, now become a revolting, pimply syphilitic.

But Pangloss is still an unchanged *tout est bien* optimist. Candide asked him, "When you were hanged, dissected, beaten black and blue, and when you were rowing in that galley, did you always think that everything in this world is for the best?" "I have not changed my mind at all," Pangloss answered. "I am a philosopher, and it would not be proper for me to do so; besides Leibniz could not have been wrong." Candide, however, had been thinking things over. He had come very bravely through his sufferings; he had never really lost heart or given up hope; but he had found that the commonly accepted worldly ways of being happy did not bring happiness. He is impressed, however, by the example of a happy and sensible Turk who kept clear of politics and all worldly affairs, knowing Constantinople only as a good market for the produce of his tiny estate. "Work without worrying," the pessimistic Martin had said; "it is the only way to make life endurable." So the little group set to work to develop their own small farm. Occasionally Pangloss would remark, "There is a chain of events in the best possible worlds. For if you had not been chased out of the Baron's castle with a kick on the bottom for making love to Miss Cunégonde; if you had not been caught by the Inquisition; if you had not wandered about America on foot; if you had not run your sword through Miss Cunégonde's brother, and lost the gold you got in Eldorado, you would not be here munching preserved fruit and pistachio nuts." "That may be quite true," Candide would reply. "Nevertheless, we have got to work in our garden." [15]

So the novel ends on this quiet note. In spite of all the evil on earth, hope does still remain, the unquenchable hope of humanity for sufficiency and contentment. One facile kind of optimism is dead, but Voltaire knows that there is another humble, tough, and resilient human optimism that no adversity can completely extinguish. It is, admittedly, a vulnerable attitude of mind; but, at least, it is always there. The prospect for mankind is not hopelessly dark, provided that we all perform our immediate duties quietly and efficiently, and undisturbed by ambition.

It is said of the Lisbon earthquake that it brought an age to an end, and in the sense that the characteristic popular optimism of the first half of the eighteenth century did not long survive the disaster, this saying is as true as any such generalization can be about so self-contradictory and complicated a subject as eighteenth-century thought. After the earthquake pessimism became a more familiar and understandable mood, while the undefeatably hopeful minds occupied themselves more and more with the idea of perfectibility, a gradual progress by man under God's providence towards a full happiness and perfection. In effecting this change, the influence of *Candide* played a significant part; indeed, what the tragedy of the Lisbon earthquake had only partly achieved

[15] On this famous passage, see the notes to Best, 185, *Voltaire's Correspondence*, I.

by the resulting emotions of horror and pity, a novel turned into a significant revolution of thought.

A young French poet gives an example of the changed outlook. When the Lisbon earthquake happened, Ponce-Denis Écouchard Le Brun, already a budding literary figure of some promise, was twenty-six. As soon as the news reached Paris he wrote a poem on the disaster that was published almost immediately, a prettily conventional piece about the folly of pride. Lisbon was overproud; now Lisbon, Queen of the Seas, is no more; puny, foolish mankind must reflect that it is God who rules the world. Then came the further news of the death of young Racine, and deeply grieved at the loss of this beloved friend, Le Brun wrote a second poem, gloomily describing the physical causes of earthquakes and the terrible effects the forces of nature can produce. God seems to be always changing the face of the world and the life upon it; He oppresses in this way sea and land and all mankind; He mocks our credulous happiness; there is ultimately no escape from the forces He has unleashed against us. Smyrna, Pompeii, Herculaneum, Lima, and now Lisbon! We are all in peril.

The world is a hard place for us poor mortals. What have they really done to deserve such miseries? Dear Racine, cries Le Brun, if my complaints can reach you in the shades, let my love for you make up for the cruel injustice of fate.

In 1761, in the middle of the Seven Years' War, Le Brun, who was newly married and had a good post and no private reasons at that time for being excessively gloomy, wrote an "Ode to the Sun on the Misfortunes of the Earth since the Lisbon earthquake in 1755." "O

Sun," he asked, "have you ever looked upon such awful horrors as those now afflicting mankind?" The earthquake at this moment seemed almost a minor disaster, for man himself had begun to join with nature in wrecking the world. There had been an attempt to assassinate King Louis XV in 1757, and also an attempt on the life of King José of Portugal in 1758, even while poor Lisbon still lay in ruins. "O Sun! When you looked down almost into Hell through the earthquake-chasms did you not see the evil spirits escaping?" Three times in this century the Turks have terrified Europe, and Europe itself is ablaze with war; from the Dneiper and the Vistula to the Thames and the Seine the rivers are crowded with assembling fleets. And consider the New World! Tyrannical Europe has inflicted every possible misery on America, and the greed of white men has destroyed the happiness of the native peoples. England is at war with us in North America; there are bloody battles in the territory where our gallant Jumonville was killed eight years ago. War destroys all the blessings that the sun gives, and gold brings equal disaster; it is because of a shameless lust for gold that African slaves are poured into Mexico.

> Ah! périsse la mémoire
> De nos lamentables jours!
> Grand Dieu! quelle ombre assez noire
> En peut absorber le cours!
> Siècle infame! siècle atroce!
> Ou l'impiété féroce
> Du ciel usurpa les droits!

The poet hopes that the sun will lead mankind to a happy existence in the Fortunate Islands, very pleasantly imagined; but we need not follow him further. It is enough to know that in the space of about six years the age of optimism had in Le Brun's opinion degenerated into the Dark Ages. The eighteenth century: *siècle infame, siècle atroce.*

Chapter Eight

LONDON, 1755-56

The news of the earthquake that had done so much harm to Lisbon travelled slowly. It took a week or ten days before it was generally known in Spain and in the near Mediterranean world, well over a fortnight to reach Paris and London, and nearly a month to get to Hamburg. In England the arrival of Sir Benjamin Keene's dispatch of 10 November from Madrid was the first intimation of what had happened. The shock of the news, as soon as the magnitude of the disaster became current talk, was so upsetting that some people at first refused to believe in what seemed to be a preposterous rumour. On 25 November, Horace Walpole wrote, "there is a most dreadful account of an earthquake in Lisbon, but several people will not believe in it," and on the following day the Duke of Bedford was informed that "the terrible report from Lisbon is not believed in the extent it is talked of." Samuel Johnson was for a long time sceptical. And the first accounts to arrive were, of course, exaggerated and contradictory. Two-thirds of the city destroyed and about one hundred thousand lives lost, was the announcement in the *London Magazine* on 26 November, but "we must wait for more exact accounts." In the December number the death-roll was given as seventy thousand, though there were only ten or twelve English casualties. In France the Duc de Luynes had information from Lisbon that the losses numbered eight thousand to thirteen thousand; but later he thought this was a deliberate understatement issued purposely in order to save the King of Portugal pain; fifty thousand was more likely. This was the figure the *Gazette de France* (22 November) had already suggested. On all sides people were thinking and talking about the earthquake, and especially about the poor King of Portugal, for the privations of King José seemed to epitomize the full horror of the earthquake. That a king should suffer thus! A letter by him to his brother-in-law, King Ferdinand VI of Spain, was quoted as showing that for the first day or two the miserable monarch did not even know if he was going to get enough to eat, a dreadful thought that made a deep impression both in England and in France.[1]

There were four practical reactions to the news, and

---

[1] The English had decided they liked King José: popular verse lavished praise on him:

> A noble palace in whose bright domain,
> A monarch loving as belov'd does reign;
> Generous, humane, who scorns the servile art,
> By ought but reason to engage the heart;
> Who knows no pleasure but his country's bliss,
> In that is centred every heart-felt wish;
>> *A Poem on the Late Earthquake at Lisbon.*
>> London, 1755.

> Lo, the good king from out the ruin'd heaps,
> By providence divine, like Lot escapes;
> .   .   .   .
> Like Job he grieved, like Job he kissed the rod,
> And own'd the justice of his angry God.
>> *A Poem on the Earthquake at Lisbon.*
>> London, 1755.

the first was charity. Religious anxiety and concern over financial losses and scientific speculation shared jointly a second place. The charity was warmhearted and immediate, for in spite of all that was so soon said about the chastisement of the wicked Lisbon people being deserved, in general people were truly sorry for the Portuguese and did not neglect their kindly duties as neighbours.[2] The King of Spain made immediate presents of money and food, and eased the frontier regulations so that the inflow of supplies would not be impeded; the King of France offered money to be minted at his expense in Portugal, an offer that was declined as was the main offer of financial assistance from Spain. Hamburg sent ships to Lisbon laden with wood, which was desperately needed, and tiles, lead, and tools and other goods that would be practically useful in the emergency, and also a little personal gift, a token present of wine and sugar, for the King. Three ships were dispatched with this necessary material on 17 December, and a fourth ship was most considerately kept in reserve to sail after Lisbon's requirements were better known. England sent money, partly in Portuguese gold coins and partly in Spanish silver dollars, meat, butter, biscuits, rice, wheat and flour, smoked herrings, boots and shoes, and picks and shovels. News that the gift was on its way reached King José at Belém on 21 December; but a few days before this, H.M.S. *Hampton Court*, carrying the money, had had to put back into Portsmouth because of bad weather, and it was not until the last day of the year that the supplies began to arrive.

There was a kindly thoughtfulness in the English gift.

---

[2] The Genoese republic seems, perhaps accidentally, to have been an exception. *Giornale Ligustico* (Anno., xiv, 1887), p. 69.

Meal and flour were included because it was feared that there might not be enough mills surviving in and close to Lisbon to grind quickly a large quantity of corn. The Earl of Halifax suggested to the Duke of Newcastle that England should send out young surgeons and doctors, and also plenty of blankets. It was Sir John Barnard, M.P. for the City of London, who first thought of sending out a good supply of ready cash. There was also a less generous suggestion that as much Irish beef as possible should be bought for Portugal, because this would be a good move against the French, suspected of wanting to use Ireland as a base for victualling their fleet. The Portuguese were greatly comforted by this kindness and insisted that destitute British in Lisbon should take a first share of the gift. A nineteenth-century opinion, "They [the Portuguese] received the English relief, but cursed the heretical hands that afforded it," [3] is a false judgement influenced by later commercial quarrels between the two nations, and stories of the wasteful mismanagement of the gift come from anti-Pombal sources and are unproven; also, there is no reason for believing Sir Benjamin Keene was right in his guess when he remarked to Castres in a letter of 16 February 1756 that he supposed that the British Factory would expect preferential treatment because of the liberality of their nation. What is quite certain is that Newcastle's Government was supported by a unanimous Parliament when, in response to His Majesty's gracious message of 28 November, Britain sent help to Portugal, generously, quickly, and with an unqualified sympathy for a friendly nation in distress.

[3] S. A. Dunham: *History of Spain and Portugal*, v, p. 257, (1832.) The author is quoting "a modern historian of Portugal."

Yet the commercial losses caused by the earthquake to nations other than the Portuguese was almost at once a matter of great concern. One of Voltaire's first thoughts on hearing the news was alarm about the fortune of his friend, Jean-Robert Tronchin, the banker of Lyons, and of the textile merchants of that city. Similarly, the heavy losses of the British Factory, both real and fancied, greatly shocked England. Mary Granville, Mrs. Delany, who was gloomily full of the noblest moral reflections on the disaster, had also time to think of her friends' financial interests. She wrote on 29 November, "Mr. Mellish's loss will be very considerable from the earthquake; he is a most worthy man; and his partner, now in England, has lost friends, fortune, family, every connection in life. Mr. Gore's loss is at least £30,000; Mr. Bristow, the merchant . . . £100,000; the Bishop of St. Asaph £7,000, part of his wife's fortune.[4] Every day will make, I fear, some new unhappy discovery." In December of the same year, 1755, the Reverend Josiah Tucker of St. Stephen's, Bristol, afterwards Dean of Gloucester, wrote, "This city of Bristol has suffered the least of any in the kingdom, considering the extent of its trade, by the late dreadful calamity at Lisbon. Only one person being concerned as an exporter of cloth, a worthy industrious parishioner of mine, who computes his loss at about £9,000." Letters from Lisbon reaching London after the earthquake understandably emphasized this aspect of the disaster, for the British Factory had indeed suffered severely; offices had been destroyed, correspondence and ledgers burnt,

[4] Robert Hay Drummond (1711-76), later Archbishop of York; his wife was the daughter of a London merchant.

money and merchandise irretrievably lost; no one could
doubt that the earthquake had done great harm to British
overseas trade, and there were many justifiable and understandable laments. The great hope was that a recovery
of Lisbon's normal facilities for trading would put all this
right. An anonymous English poet understood the position. Rebuked by his muse for questioning God's wholesale slaughtering of the Portuguese without warning, at a
time when many of these unfortunate people were doubtless

> Unfit to stand their Audit dread,
> With all their crimes upon their Head,
> Perhaps, *full-blown* as May!

he was told to think of the future and was granted a
vision of Lisbon recovered from the disaster. Buildings
are being erected; merchandise is pouring into the splendid new city; the harbour is crowded with boats; there
is a pocket-filling economic boom:

> The Sons of Commerce fill the Street,
> In Hymns their great Restorer greet,
> And hail reviving Trade.

Side by side with the mercenary consideration, there
was much fact-collecting and theorizing by scientists who
did their best to account for the earthquake according to
the seismological theories then current. Led by the Royal
Society, there was a creditable and a very prolific inquiry,
and John Bevis's *History and Philosophy of Earthquakes*,
the best known of the scientific publications of the time,
is a notable corpus of seismological material, containing
much useful contemporary information about the earth-

quake of 1 November 1755.[5] But the effect of the news that most of all concerns this chapter and the chief interest of this book is the religious consternation that so quickly made itself apparent in England, as indeed in other European countries.

People were seriously perturbed and felt that a solemn supernatural message had been delivered to them. Possibly, this consternation was felt more generally in England than elsewhere on the Continent. Treaty quarrels and religious differences did not diminish England's basic affection for Lisbon and the Portuguese; many Englishmen knew Portugal well and had lived happily there, or had friends who had done so; the nation had no such close ties with any other independent foreign country. Samuel Richardson wrote on 15 December 1755, "What dreadful news we have from Lisbon. The only city in the world,

[5] Published, London, 1757. The work is described as by "a member of the Royal Academy of Berlin." Another useful study is *An Historical Account of Earthquakes*, Liverpool, 1756, by an anonymous author, published with the Fast-Day sermon of Thomas Hunter of Weversham, Cheshire, but not by him. A curious paper well worth reading is John Winthrop's *A Lecture on Earthquakes; read in the Chapel of Harvard College in Cambridge, N.E., November 26th, 1755 on an occasion of the great Earthquake which shook New-England the week before* (Boston, 1755). Winthrop was Professor of Mathematics and Philosophy, and his subject was an earthquake of 18 November that "so lately spread terror, and threatened desolation throughout New-England." It does not seem to have done very much harm apart from breaking the spindle of the vane on Faneuil Hall in Boston, but it created the usual consternation in full measure. Winthrop, however, had a good deal to say in favour of earthquakes; they may be "of real and standing advantage to the globe in general." They destroy multitudes, but much greater multitudes may have been every day benefited by them. They loosen and disunite the parts of the earth, and open its pores. They should be compared with ploughing and the breaking up of the clods of earth. This view ought to silence all complaints of sufferers and the objections of sceptics. We are, said Winthrop, "in a mix'd state." Nothing is simply and absolutely evil.

out of the British dominions, by which so tremendous a shock could have so much affected us. When the Almighty's judgements are abroad, may we be warned." This is a statement of the normal reaction of the Englishman to the news of the Lisbon earthquake, just as part of Isaiah xxvi. 9 was many times chosen as the appropriate text for a sermon on this occasion: "for when thy judgments are in the earth, the inhabitants of the world will learn righteousness."

Moralizing poured forth in speech and writing. "What a scene is this," Mrs. Delany continued in her letter of 29 November, "to awaken those who think of nothing but greatness and wealth! and to those of a better turn it will, I hope, strengthen their pursuit after immortal happiness." She was aware that not everybody kept such noble reflections persistently in mind. "Can those wretches at Whites," she asked on Boxing Day, "read [sad accounts of more earthquakes] like common paragraphs of news? Surely no: at least it is to be hoped they cannot; and yet I fear that those who least stand in need of such warnings are most touched by them."

This was probably a harsh judgement, as the wretches at White's may have been just as shocked by the earthquake news as Mrs. Delany. The young Captain Augustus Hervey, afterwards third Earl of Bristol, who had recently had a most gloriously happy time at Lisbon, would certainly have been considered by Mrs. Delany, had she known of his goings-on, as a wretch deplorably in need of warning; but, when he got the news at Malta, he wrote in his diary, "The next day, the 9th, we had the sad news of the fatal earthquake that happened at Lisbon, with many particulars of that misfortune, and that it had been felt in many places of Europe, and even across the ocean to Barbary. . . . These are frightful events, and ought to inspire reflections that should mend the lives of individuals in order not to deserve such chastisements from Providence." [6] It cannot be said that the gallant sailor himself made an impresive show of reform; but his immediate sadness was genuine and his sentiment sincere.

The earthquake did produce, however, a marked change in people's behaviour, lasting at any rate for some months. Dr. Law, the Vice-Chancellor of Cambridge University, wrote from Peterhouse on 20 January 1756 to the Duke of Newcastle, "We have been perfectly quiet here, nor have I had any certain information of the least irregularity among the scholars. It is rather become fashionable to be decent." After the public Fast-Day in February 1756 Horace Walpole wrote to Henry Seymour Conway, "Between the French and the Earthquake you have no notion how good we are grown; nobody makes a suit now but of sackcloth turned up with ashes." The fast was kept so devoutly, that Dick Edgecumbe, finding a very lean hazard at White's, said with a sigh, "Lord, how the times are degenerated! Formerly a fast would have brought everybody hither; now it keeps everybody away." Ordinary folk and not only the clergy were much upset when a masquerade was advertised to take place at the Haymarket Theatre towards the end of January. The announcement was an affront to the nation's mood, the Bishop of London told Newcastle on 20 January; the Duke agreed, and he went at once to ask the King to

[6] *Augustus Hervey's Journal*, ed. David Erskine, p. 189. London, 1953.

stop the ball, which was done, the King having also received a protest from the Archbishop of Canterbury.

Walpole was full of gossip on this subject of reformed characters, not always accurate, but shrewdly sensing the earthquake-mood. Even the fascinating speculation about the Pompadour's rouge took an earthquake-turn.

In France the prosecution of the war was by no means an unanimous measure. D'Argenson, the promoter of it, was on ill terms with Madame Pompadour whose interest was to lull the King and nation in pleasures and inactivity, not to foment events that might shake her power. It received a blow from another quarter. The Cardinal de la Rochfoucault and Sassy,[7] the King's Confessor, played off the earthquake on his superstition. He promised to receive the sacrament at Easter, and relinquish his mistress. She, who held more by habit than passion, saw no reason why a woman might not work the machine of religion as well as a priest, and instantly gave in to all his Majesty's scruples; offered up her *rouge* to the demon of earthquakes, and to sanctify her conversion and reconcile it to Court-life, procured herself to be declared Dame du Palais to the Queen.[8]

The best-known comment on the effects produced by the preaching and moralizing after the earthquake was that of Goethe, recalling his childhood. "The peace of mind of a little boy [he was just over six years old] was for the first time most profoundly disturbed by an event

[7] Père de Sacy, a Jesuit.
[8] *Memoirs of the Reign of King George II* (second edition, 1847), ɪɪ, p. 176.

of worldwide significance." The Lisbon earthquake, Goethe said, startled a more or less quiet and happy society with a sudden terror, and he described the horrible nature of the event with its reputed sixty thousand casualties, and he told of the alarm caused in Germany and elsewhere by reports of earth-tremors and the disturbance of waters all over Europe. "Thereafter came a swarm of theories from the pious, consolatory opinions from the philosophers, and threatening sermons from the clergy." The whole world was afraid.

Perhaps never before has the Demon of Fright so quickly and so powerfully spread horror throughout the land. The little boy, who heard everybody talking about the event, was deeply impressed. God, the creator and preserver of heaven and earth, God, said to be omniscient and merciful, had shown himself to be a very poor sort of father, for he had struck down equally the just and the unjust. In vain the young mind sought to combat this idea; but it was clear that even learned theologians could not agree about the way in which to account for such a disaster.

"Embarrassing for the professors of physics and humiliating for the theologians" had been a first comment of Edmond-Jean Barbier, the Parisian lawyer and diary-writer, when he heard of the great earthquake. It was a shrewd judgement. The scientists puzzled everybody with the variety of their theories about the physical causes of an earthquake, and the theologians found themselves in a confusion of attack and defence, anxious on the one hand to use the earthquake as a rebuke to sin, and forced on the other hand to justify such an indiscriminately savage act of a supposedly loving God. The clergy had to preach to a cowed and at the same time a questioning congregation.

There were a number of very peculiar views expressed, and the laity had plenty to say as well as the parsons. In England, for example, a Member of Parliament, who was an Old Testament scholar, and presumably an admirer of Warburton's *Divine Legation,* demanded a return to the philosophy of Moses, who, he said, was a much wiser man than either Descartes or Newton. The world was paying now for its neglect of Moses's teaching. What were the autos-da-fé of Portugal but orgies of human sacrifice conducted "amidst the acclamation of the most ignorant and bigotted race of men that ever pretended to the name of Christians"? Moses had condemned idolatry, but idolatry was rampant in Portugal where the Supreme Being could be seen represented in the figure of an old man. Images of "He and She Saints" crowded the churches, and incense and genuflexions honour these senseless blocks of wood. And though God is at the moment punishing disobedience to the Mosaic rule in Portugal how do we know that His earthquakes will not progress round the whole globe, destroying us on the way? For the English are every bit as bad in their neglect of Moses's teaching; they are corrupt, and have an insatiable appetite for amusements like cards and the theatre; they live in the idlenes of a Sodom they have made for themselves. Read what Gildas said about the Britons before they were overrun by the Saxons, and see if that scathing denunciation does not fit the Britons of the present day. Back then at once to the proper austerity of the rule of Moses.[9]

It was easy enough in a Protestant country to heap reproaches upon poor Lisbon. Lisbon, stated the *London Magazine* succinctly, "might be said to be at once the most visibly rich, and the most abandonedly wicked and superstitious city in the world." A "Clergyman at London," addressing words of comfort to "the remaining disconsolate inhabitants of Lisbon," told them that in spite of all their religious magnificence and their show of devotion they had "surpassed the whole world in wickedness"; "is there," he asked them, "a scene of lewdness or debauchery that was ever practised which hath not been daily repeated in your religious houses?" And as for murder, a Lisbon priest could be hired as an assassin for a mere trifle. The Inquisition; the idols; what could be worse? "If you have not entirely lost your reason, by being debarred the use of it," you should now ask yourselves how God could possibly overlook your wicked be-

[9] *Reflections Physical and Moral upon the various . . . Phenomena . . . which have happened from the Earthquake at Lima, to the present time. In a series of Familiar Letters from a Member of Parliament in Town to his Friend in the Country* (London, 1756). The author was probably James Dawkins (1722-57), a wealthy young Jacobite, M.P. for Hindon, Wiltshire, who was born in Jamaica; in the course of a short life he had travelled widely, and it was he who accompanied Robert Wood to Palmyra and Balbec. I owe this identification to the kindness of Sir Lewis Namier and Mr. John Brooke of the History of Parliament Trust. Another curiosity of the period is the *Earnest Address* to the people of this country by Alexander Cruden (1701-70), author of the *Biblical Concordance,* "the Corrector" appointed by heaven to censor the morals of the British. He was at this time petitioning the House of Commons to introduce his Bill for the "Reformation of the People," and he wrote to the Duke of Newcastle to point out that the Lisbon earthquake and the threat of war with France made it more than ever urgent to get his Bill passed.

haviour, and do not let there be any grumbling talk about the innocent perishing with the guilty; there were no really innocent people in Lisbon. And, "if any English residents remain," let them ask themselves if they were not miserably debauched and unworthy Protestants, gambling and drinking, and cheating at business just like the dishonest traders among whom they lived. "I am sorry to say it is a known truth that the English in general which composed our several factories abroad are far from doing honour to the Christian character by their exemplary lives." The Lisbon priests, with particularly unsympathetic injustice, were sternly denounced. One writer [10] accused them of telling falsehoods, and even fathering them upon God Himself, in order to plunder the earthquake victims. As for the Inquisitors, "the hottest Hell," said a preacher in Staffordshire, "will undoubtedly be their portion." [11]

It was, most of all, the cruelty of the Inquisition that even the merciful could not put out of their minds; blood-guiltiness it was called (Pl. VIII). John Wesley asked:

> Is there indeed a God that judges the world, and is he now making an Inquisition for Blood? If so, it is not surprising he should begin there [Lisbon] where so much blood has been poured on the ground like water? Where so many brave men have been murdered, in the most base and cowardly, as well as barbarous manner almost every day, as well as every night, while none regarded or laid it to heart. . . . How long has their blood been crying from the earth? Yea, how long has that bloody *House of Mercy,* the scandal not only

---

[10] S. Hayward: *Letter to the Inhabitants of Great Britain.* London, 1756.

[11] R. Watkins: *Fast-Day Sermon,* p. 13. Clifton Campville, Staffs.

of all religion, but even of human nature, stood to insult both heaven and earth? [12]

After the Inquisition, came idolatry and after that Portugal's abject devotion to wealth. "Think, O Spain, O Portugal of the millions of poor Indians that your forefathers butchered for the sake of gold." [13] Sometimes there is a note of condescension in this type of denunciation. "The Portuguese nation is remarked for many vices, though in some qualities they are praiseworthy and some instances of piety and virtue there are without doubt among them; yet, in general, treachery and revenge, covetousness and usury, theft, and frequent murders, and above all most inhuman cruelty, are the character of that people." [14] There is also an occasional note of self-satisfaction. "And when all the lofty temples and other Popish religious houses have been thrown down and laid in ruins, a single Protestant chapel, the only one in the place, hath been left standing." [15] And again, "Let us here observe the distinguishing arm of God, how effectually he separates from these objects of his displeasure those who are influenced by Christian principles; how, in their behalf, he says unto destruction, thus far shalt thou go, and no farther; how Protestants, who are safe in harbour, have His favour a sanctuary on every side of them." [16]

[12] *Serious Thought occasioned by the late Earthquake at Lisbon*, pp. 4, 5. Second edition, Bristol, 1755. Wesley confused the Inquisition with the Casa da Misericórdia.

[13] Thomas Hartley, Rector of Winwick, Northants: *God's Controversy with the Nations*, p. 15. London, 1756.

[14] R. Watkins: *Fast-Day Sermon*, p. 7. Clifton Campville, Staffs.

[15] Thomas Alcock preaching at St. Andrew, Plymouth, 31 December 1755 and 4 February 1756.

[16] *Exhortation . . . unto the People of London occasion'd by the late Proclamation for a Fast*. By a Clergyman of Gloucestershire, p. 26. London, 1756.

Yet most preachers in England were neither smug nor unrelentingly hardhearted. Thomas Alcock (1709-98), who commented on the survival of the Protestant chapel, did go on to say that such arguments really meant nothing at all. "If Popish superstition and cruelty made Lisbon fall, how came Rome to stand?" He asked if a Portuguese bigot was really any worse an offender against God than an English infidel or atheist? The Portuguese have at least, he said, "a zeal of God," and he described them as punctual and honest in their dealings, and by their trade and alliance extremely beneficial to this nation. "Their Royal family are decent and generally wellspoken of." Alcock truly represented his Church in taking as his text, as so many of his fellow-clergy did, Luke xiii, 2-5:

And Jesus answering said unto them, Suppose ye that these Galileans were sinners above all the Galileans, because they suffered such things? I tell you, Nay: but, except ye repent, ye shall all likewise perish. Or those eighteen, upon whom the tower in Siloam fell, and slew them, think ye that they were sinners above all men that dwelt in Jerusalen? I tell you, Nay: but, except ye repent, ye shall all likewise perish.

In fact, even the most ferocious denouncers of Lisbon wickedness usually went on to make it plain to their hearers that though the sins of the unlucky inhabitants of that city were scandalous, even more shocking and abominable were the sins of their own nation. What, for instance, in these special circumstances could be more deplorable than the behaviour of some of the refugees from the earthquake, or better illustrate the general depravity of the British? A party of them, whose obvious duty it was to spend their first hours on return to their own country in humble thanksgiving, arrived in Falmouth when the church bells were ringing and, instead of going to say their prayers, they went to a tavern, sent for whores and two fiddlers, and spent the night in riot and debauchery.[17]

The whole nation was easily shown to be in a miserable state of sin. "When was there less Fidelity amongst Mankind? When was there less *brotherly love?* When was *gratitude* less practised? When were *Murmurings* more frequent? *Malice* more powerful? *Envy* more subtil? Vengeance more active? Or *Hatred* more rooted in us?"[18] Drunkenness, perjury, profanity, desecration of the Sabbath: "people of any consequence in civil life would be ashamed to be seen at church, especially at the sacraments; and, if they want to go a journey, no day so convenient and agreeable as the Sunday."[19] Protestants had won the precious right to read the Bible; they shamefully neglected the opportunity. In this country there is "such an affront offered by us to Christ, as the heathen do not offer to their idols, nor the Papists to their superstitions."[20] Cards, dice, the theatre, dancing, gluttony, adultery, sodomy: "this nation has well-nigh filled up the measures of its iniquities."[21] We are "a discontented, fractious, ungrateful, divided people."[22] "It is almost a fashion

[17] T. Jones: *Fast-Day Sermon,* p. 10. St. Saviour, Southwark.
[18] Isaac Nieto (Netto): *Fast-Day Sermon,* p. 6. Portuguese Jews' Synagogue.
[19] Webster: *Fast-Day Sermon,* p. 26. Ware, Herts.
[20] Samuel Walker: *Fast-Day Sermon,* p. 11. Truro.
[21] T. Jones: Sermon, 1 February 1756, p. 8. St. Saviour, Southwark.
[22] James How: *Fast-Day Sermon,* p. 18. Milton-next-Gravesend, Kent.

to be thought wicked." [23] What is to be expected of a nation that habitually sends its youth to Popish countries for improvement? Heresies are flourishing; a bold licentious spirit of criticism newly sprung up, declares the Scriptures to be uncertain and subject to correction.[24] Religion is subject to banter, ridicule, and sophistry; it is persistently undermined by deism. Even the clergy are culpable, many of them being imprudent, indiscreet, slothful, and idle. Britain's case was hard indeed, and there was no time left. "Tomorrow's sun may never rise upon us; this night may plunge us into the sleep of death . . . every word I speak, and every breath you draw, may be our last." [25]

The people listened to a storm of warnings and threats from their pastors. God "comes with many signal strokes of vengeance to awaken a careless and sleepy world," said William Romaine, Lecturer at St. Dunstan-in-the-West, on 30 November, preaching to the text, "Prepare to meet thy God." Most of them were seriously frightened, but not all of them were frightened enough. On 14 December this fine man had to speak more plainly to the people. God

has arisen to shake terribly the earth, you are not moved. He has come to take vengeance on a guilty race, and has punished them with a most exemplary destruction, but you are not affected. . . . This strange stupidity and hardness of your hearts will soon bring down some heavy calamity upon you.

[23] John Fountayne, Dean of York: *Fast-Day Sermon*, p. 25.
[24] Daniel Gittins: *Fast-Day Sermon*, p. 27. South Stoke, Sussex, and Leominster.
[25] Thomas Hunter: *Fast-Day Sermon*, p. 17. Weversham, Cheshire.

Another writer cried:

> Wo unto thee Britain; wo unto thee Ireland; wo unto
> thee London; wo unto thee Liverpool; for if the in-
> structions, the admonitions, the warnings, the counsels,
> which have from God been given unto you, in the pure
> preaching of the Gospel, had been given to Lisbon, it
> would long ago have repented and turned from all its
> abominations, and remained to this day. Therefore it
> shall be more tolerable for that ruined city in the Day
> of Judgment than for you.[26]

But all this was not part of the message that the Church
of England delivered in a responsible corporate voice; the
Church asked of its people a change of heart, and one
of the official measures taken in order to give opportunity
for a serious effort to understand what the Church had
to say was the appointment by royal proclamation on 18
December 1755 of Friday, 6 February 1756, as a general
Fast-Day. There had been many of these days of public
intercession and repentance before, mostly with the self-
ishly national intention that such occasions tend to have,
and 6 February was no exception, for fear of the approaching war with France had been added to the fear
of a great earthquake like that which had destroyed Lisbon. But even so the traditional wording of the proclamation is impressive.

> Whereas the manifold Sins and Wickedness of these
> Kingdoms, have most justly deserved heavy and severe
> punishments from the Hand of Heaven; and the Al-

---

[26] *An Historical Account of Earthquakes*, p. 129. Liverpool, 1756. This
lively anonymous work is published with Thomas Hunter's *Fast-Day Sermon* preached at Weversham, Cheshire, and is attributed to him; but
there is strong internal evidence that the *Account* is not by Hunter.

mighty, out of His great Mercy, hath not only been our Defence in Times of Danger, but hath protected and preserved Us from imminent Destruction, especially at this Time, when some neighbouring Countries, in Alliance and Friendship with Us, have been visited with a most dreadful and extensive Earthquake, which hath also, in some Degree, been felt in several Parts of Our Dominions:

a public fast is to be observed in England and Wales, as also by separate proclamations in Scotland and Ireland.

The proclamation ordered that special forms of prayer should be published for the occasion. The principal collect in the form for public use is a petition that expresses exactly the theological significance of the Lisbon earthquake as it was generally understood and accepted in the eighteenth century:

we, vile dust and miserable sinners, in a most awful sense of thy amazing power . . . beseech thee, O Lord, to awaken our consciences yet farther, that we may see and duly consider thy hand, which, in the most astonishing manner, hath been lifted up so near us. Pardon those crying sins, which have produced these tokens of thy heavy displeasure, and grant us all such a measure of thy grace, that we may no more disobey thy laws, abuse thy forbearance, or despise thy chastisements, lest a worse thing come upon us. It is of thy goodness, O Lord, that we were not all consumed, when thou didst arise to shake terribly the earth, and that in the midst of judgement, thou didst remember mercy. Let the deep sense of this work in us such a thankfulness of heart . . . that no calamity may surprise us, nor death itself come upon us unawares, and that we may at length arrive at that blessed Kingdom, which cannot be shaken. . . . Amen.

A large number of the Fast-Day sermons have been printed, and all of them have a central message calling for repentance and a change of heart. *"Thou also shall perish. Behold me smoking! Remember and* REPENT. This is the short but very full sermon that Lisbon in ruins preaches to London in sin." [27] It was the proper theme for the occasion, and it was an expected message. "The public fast was observed with a becoming decency by all ranks of people. The churches and meeting-houses were thronged, and there was, in appearance, an entire cessation from business throughout the city and suburbs, and all over the kingdom." [28] The public mood dictated the preacher's discourse; but the Fast-Day sermons were nevertheless mostly fine and original messages of conscientious pastors, and understandably so, for, preached as they generally were to crowded congregations of attentive and apprehensive people, these sermons had to be the very best the preachers could prepare to fit so important an occasion.

As an example, here is the substance of a sermon preached on the Fast-Day at St. Paul's, Deptford, by the rector, James Bate (1703-75), of Corpus, Cambridge. The Lisbon earthquake, he said, "exceeds anything in history"

[27] George Horne: *Fast-Day Sermon*, p. 19. Oxford (City and University). Horne was Fellow of Magdalen, and later President, and afterwards Bishop of Norwich; the Lisbon earthquake happened on his twenty-fifth birthday.

[28] *London Magazine*, vol. xxv (February 1756). Three houses of the Quakers in Lombard Street kept open and caused great affront, so much so that in the afternoon an indignant crowd broke their windows. *Public Advertiser*, 7 February 1756.

except the Flood, and we have to reckon with the frightening fact that our own island has subterranean caverns beneath its surface that could easily produce a similar disaster here. But we do not understand "the Councils of God," and we do not know what is going to happen. "It is God alone who can dart his eye through futurity," and all we can be sure of is that He has adapted the "machine of the Universe" to answer all His purposes. Earthquakes are part of His plan; but we have to remember that this world is not a place of retribution, but a place of probation, for God usually punishes sinners not *here* but *hereafter;* therefore the sufferers in an earthquake are not necessarily very evil people, and in the case of the Lisbon earthquake we must recognize that God is speaking to us all. The plain fact is that God has now no other way of bringing us to our senses than by frightening us; that is the purpose of this really dreadful calamity. Let us then heed this obvious warning and humbly acknowledge that we must immediately and genuinely mend our ways. Yet our peril does not mean that we must despair. We are not a hopelessly bad people; we have been very generous to Portugal; we are improving in loyalty to our Hanoverian King; we appreciate our present Government; we tolerate dissenting Protestant brethren, and our increasing political solidarity is adding to the confusion of the encroaching, falsehearted and perfidious French.

In this multitude of sermons, alike in kind, but surprisingly varied, indeed sometimes contradictory in emphasis and detail, it is to the credit of the preachers that nearly all have some strong individual character. For another example there is the opinion of the learned and truculently argumentative William Warburton (1698-

1779), afterwards Bishop of Gloucester, who in 1756 was a royal chaplain and preacher at Lincoln's Inn, where he delivered his Fast-Day sermon.

Warburton had had something to say about the Lisbon earthquake before he preached his Fast-Day sermon in Lincoln's Inn Chapel. He thought that the calamity had not really produced the effect it should have done, and on 9 December 1755 he wrote:

> Time was, when the imaginary displeasures of Heaven in a comet or an eclipse have disarmed warring nations when their swords were already lifted up for mutual slaughter. But I do not hear that these marks of divine displeasure on a sinful people are likely to abate our and our neighbours animosities against one another.[29]

To Richard Hurd, also in December 1755, he said:

> To suppose these desolutions the scourge of heaven for human impieties, is a dreadful reflection; and yet to suppose ourselves in a forlorn and fatherless world, is ten times a more frightful consideration. In the first case, we may reasonably hope to avoid our destruction by the amendment of our manners; in the latter we are kept incessantly alarmed by the blind rage of warring elements.[30]

But Warburton also wondered whether the significance of the disaster was overestimated.

> And yet does not human pride make us miscalculate? A drunken man shall work as horrid a desolation with the kick of his foot against an ant-hill, as subterraneous air and fermented minerals, to a populous city. And if

[29] Letter to Joseph Atwell: *Works*, xiv, p. 257. London, 1841.
[30] Warburton-Hurd Letters, lxxxvii.

we take in the universe of things, rather with a philosophic than a religious eye, where is the difference in point of real importance between them?

The only difference lies in the merits of the two societies, for "the little Troglodytes" are superior to men in organisation, behaviour, and industry; and in a passage of bitter pessimism Warburton rejected the view that the *sovereignty of Reason* gave man the advantage over the ants.

> To this I reply, that the common definition of man is false: he is not a *reasoning animal*. The best you can predict of him is, that he is an *animal capable of reason,* and this too we take upon old tradition. For it has not been my fortune yet to meet, I don't say with any one man, but I may safely swear with any order of men, who ever did reason.

Warburton's Fast-Day sermon has the title *National and Civil Events the Instruments of God's Moral Government.* God, our moral governor, must be expected to make His dominion manifest in any way He likes in whatever kind of world He has been pleased to station His accountable and probationary creatures, and in inflicting upon the world a great disaster it must be ordinarily assumed that whether or no the disaster is a direct punishment on a particular people for a particular offence, it is quite certainly a warning to all mankind. The truth is that great general calamities, which must be accepted as evidence of God's displeasure at our sins, in fact display "his glory in the fairest colours" and help to establish "man's peace and happiness on the most lasting foundations"; for to maintain, as was fashionable, that an earthquake had nothing to do with God's moral government is simply to increase the disquiet and alarm of miserable mankind thus abandoned by Providence. But if the cause of natural events is pre-established in relation to a moral government of the world, heresies such as that of Manichaean "evil principle" that has a share in the direction of the universe, are shown to be ridiculous, and a pious person has a comforting glimpse of the generous wisdom of God's rule. For it *is* a comforting thing to know that a sincere purpose of amending public manners can avert an approaching act of divine vengeance. The action and prayers of good men have their part in the "pre-established harmony" which God has willed to exist between moral actions and natural events.

Such were the Fast-Day sermons, and the general lesson allowed no misunderstanding. The Almighty's judgements were abroad in the world, and the inhabitants of the world must therefore learn righteousness. *Except ye repent, ye shall all likewise perish.* It was for the times a fair and sensible message, for the clergy did not have to persuade a sceptical congregation that God was operating through the earthquake; on the contrary, a large majority of the people who came crowding into the churches were there because they were guiltily sure that God was indeed threatening them. Nevertheless, the religious argument following upon the Lisbon earthquake in England is not a plain quarrel between philosophers who thought that earthquakes were natural events and theologians who thought they were direct actions of an angry God; for there intruded here, more than it did in the Latin countries, the controversial element of religious enthusiasm. An orthodox Anglican disputed two, as it seemed to him, equally wrong views, protesting against "One set of men, who, influenced by superstition rather than benevolence, had taken greater liberties with the judgments of God than was consistent with the amiable spirit of Christianity"; and against another party, who, "more free indeed from religious Enthusiasm than licentious prejudices, had taken occasion from the late calamity to treat the notion of a providential interposition with very indecent mockery." On the one hand, insulting libertinism, on the other hand, "a spirit of malevolent enthusiasm" that had "hurried many persons to conclusions very uncharitable and . . . unwarrantable." [31]

This conflict among the God-fearing is occasionally mentioned in the Fast-Day sermons. The Bishop of Exeter, George Lavington (1684-1762), a resolute enemy of any sort of religious enthusiasm, preaching in the Cathedral, having said all the right things about justifiable fear of God's punishment and the urgent need for repentance, warned his people against exaggerated dread and hysterical panic. God's good providence would still deliver us if each individual contributed his share to a national improvement in behaviour. Men were not to be terrified out of their wits by earthquake-fright, but must continue to perform their normal duties calmly and sensibly, refusing to be driven crazy by apocalyptic alarms and wild stories about Christ's immediate advent. It is foolish to make the earthquake just "a shuddering topic of conversation." Men must not be abjectly afraid of the end of the world and of prodigies and portents. There is something within ourselves, said the Bishop, more peril-

[31] Peter Peckard: *Dissertation on Rev. XI. 13*, pp. i, 41. London, 1756.

ous than any fancied threats, namely the heavy sum of natural wickedness. *That* is the evil from which we must instantly fly.

An example of the kind of thing the Bishop of Exeter so much disliked was the popular and fast-selling pamphlet by John Wesley, *Serious Thoughts occasioned by the late Earthquake at Lisbon,* first published in London in 1755 and kept on the market in at least six editions. Wesley said it was directed not "to the small vulgar, but the great—to the learned, rich, and honourable heathens, commonly called Christians," and He was determined to give them a fright they would not easily forget. People who believe in God, he said, believe the Almighty is not well pleased with the scandalous behaviour of these heathens, for that is what they really are, and think He has shown His anger very plainly. How many hundred thousand men have lost their lives in war during the last half-century in Europe alone? Think of the dreadful earthquakes at Port Royal in Jamaica, at Lima in Peru, and at Catania in Sicily, especially Catania, where "not so much as one Lot escaped out of Sodom." Then Lisbon. Many think the British too have been under the lash in their own country. We have had civil war (the '45), a cattle-plague, and the recent affair of Whiston Cliffs in Yorkshire, where there had been alarming earth-tremors and falls of rock. Wesley had been to see the effects of the great landslide here in March 1755, and he wondered how England dare ignore such a portentous warning. No natural causes could account for his phenomenon; it was plainly God's work. Wesley turned angrily upon the presumptuous people who thought earthquakes and related events were accidents of nature. To think this is demonstrably absurd on the authority of Scripture, and the theory is "extremely uncomfortable"; for if it were true, what hope is left for mankind? We are left defenceless in the power of the elements; there is no help for us. In a splendid passage Wesley took the example of an earthquake:

> It comes! The Roof trembles! The Beams crack! The Ground rocks to and fro! Hoarse Thunder resounds from the Bowels of the Earth! And all these are but the Beginning of Sorrows. Now what Help? What Wisdom can prevent? What Strength resist the Blow? What Money can purchase, I will not say Deliverance, but an Hour's Reprieve? Poor honourable Fool, where are now thy Titles? Wealthy Fool, where is now thy golden God. If any Thing can help, it must be Prayer. But what wilt thou pray to? Not to the God of Heaven: you suppose him to have nothing to do with Earthquakes.

Wesley piled on the horror. Supposing we do not after all have an earthquake, "what think you of a comet?" What inded if Halley's comet burns the earth up in 1758! Remorselessly this powerful man hounded his readers into their duty of praying to God to save them, of fitting themselves to pray. Only a good Christian can be happy, for even if we are unhurt by storms, lightnings, earthquakes, and comets, "yet there is another grim enemy at the door. And you cannot drive him away. It is Death." But the Christian does not even fear death, for it is the gate to the glories of Eternity; "he is so far from looking upon death as an enemy, that he longs to feel his welcome embrace. He groans (but they are pleasing groans) to have Mortality swallowed up in Life."

It was magnificent, passionate exhortation, but it was the kind of thing that makes some people more embarrassed than impressed. There was, in fact, a stony resistance to enthusiasm, and there were Anglicans who preferred quieter, calmer thoughts than this sort of vigorous sermonizing reflects. One of them was the ailing Archbishop of Canterbury, Thomas Herring (1693-1757), who, if one may guess at his opinion from some references to the wording of the royal proclamation in his correspondence with his chaplain, did not attach undue importance to the Fast-Day. He had been sent John Wesley's pamphlet, and privately, in a letter to his friend William Duncombe, he said this:

> The author, in my opinion, with good parts and learning, is a most dark and saturnine creature. His pictures may frighten weak people, that, at the same time, are wicked, but I fear he will make few converts, except for a day. I have read his *Serious Thoughts,* but, for my own part, I think the rising and the setting of the sun is a more durable argument for religion than all the extraordinary convulsions of nature put together. Let a man be good on right principles, and then *impavidum ferient ruinae;* so far Horace was as good a preacher as any of us. For myself, I own I have no constitution for these frights and fervors; if I can but keep up to the regular practice of a Christian life, upon Christian reasons, I shall be in no pain for futurity, nor do I think it an essential part of religion to be pointed at for any foolish singularities.

No enthusiasm. Many clergy of the Church of England must have shared the feelings of the Archbishop of Canterbury and the Bishop of Exeter. "A presumptuous for-

wardness in pronouncing on extraordinary events we leave
to raving designing monks, methodists, and ignorant en-
thusiasts." [32] They thought that the religious significance
of the dreadful event in Lisbon and the alarm caused
everywhere by the news of what had happened must not
be estimated in a hotly emotional mood of earthquake-
fright or distorted by the exultant triumph of a satisfied
prophet of woe. London had not suffered as Lisbon had
suffered. We must thank God for that. And clearly Londoners, and all the British, must accept a sharp warning
from the Portuguese disaster. We must become a better
and more truly Christian people. But there the matter
must stop. We cannot answer the question, "Wherefore
hath the Lord done thus unto this great city?" unless it
be to warn us all, because we dare not accuse others of
being sinners above all men. In short, we do not know
why God allowed Lisbon to be destroyed. The great sermons of Élie Bertrand in Switzerland had summed up all
that eighteenth-century Protestant preachers had to say.
God is holy, so we must be afraid of Him. God is loving
and God is unchanging, so we must trust Him; even now
when Lisbon lies in ruins. No English sermon said this
so well. But Thomas Herring in his gentle way put it all
in a single sentence, "Let a man be good on right principles, and then *impavidum ferient ruinae.*" Here is no
consolation for the bereaved; no explanation of the deaths
of innocent people. We do not understand. But, even so,
a good Christian should be in no pain for futurity. Psalm
XLVI: "God is our hope and strength: a very present help

[32] Anon. (? S. Letsome): *Fast-Day Sermon. The Power of God over
the Constitution of Nature—with a dedication to the younger part of the
Town,* p. 30, footnote.

in trouble. Therefore will we not fear, though the earth be moved: and though the hills be carried into the midst of the sea." In a form of private and family prayers for the Fast-Day this was turned into a hymn "recommended to parents for their children to learn by heart, in order to impress on their tender minds an awful sense of their Creator's omnipotence in the late melancholy destruction of Lisbon."

> Tho' Earth her ancient Seat forsake,
>   By Pangs convulsive torn,
> Tho' her self-balanced Fabrick shake,
>   And ruin'd Nature mourn:

> Tho' Hills be in the Ocean lost,
>   With all their trembling Load,
> No Fear shall e'er disturb the Just,
>   Or shake his Trust in God.

Few converts "except for a day." The Archbishop was right. Very quickly the earthquake alarm and the Fast-Day mood of repentance changed into different despondencies. War broke out; there were other things to think about, and the country slipped back into its old habits. "I am still alarmed about the invasion, but don't find people are so apprehensive as at first," Mrs. Delany was writing on 1 April 1756. "Earthquakes are forgotten, assemblies and balls go on as briskly as if no such warning had been given; indeed, if we stop there it might be innocent, but luxury of all kinds and gaming run higher than ever." This illuminating comment was not entirely accurate, for some obdurate pleasure-lovers were still mourning London's most notorious earthquake victim, the Masquerade; "we have never recovered masquerades since the earthquake at Lisbon," said Horace Walpole in 1762. But, generally, Mrs. Delany was reporting the situation correctly. By the early summer of 1756 the Lisbon earthquake had lost in England its first tremendous emotional significance; it had become a memory, a memory of an awful event that was kept fresh by a stream of accounts of the state of the ruined city and of its rebuilding from British merchants and visitors in Portugal.

This memory, however, survived for a very long time in the common consciousness because, quite apart from the last chapter's story of the death of optimism, the Lisbon earthquake was a frequently mentioned event familiar to one and all, like other generally well-known facts in history. In England the "Adventures of Alphonso after the Destruction of Lisbon" in Lady Sarah Pennington's *Letters on Different Subjects* were being read in 1767 and afterwards, and Oliver Goldsmith introduced the earthquake into the dialogue of *The Good Natur'd Man* (1768) as a topical allusion that everybody in the theatre would understand. Mr. Braddock's exciting eyewitness account of the disaster was printed, long after its writer's death, in Charles Davy's *Letters . . . upon Subjects of Literature* in 1787. There are many other references.

It is not easy to say when the Lisbon earthquake became almost forgotten history, but it was probably before Teodoro de Almeida published *Lisboa Destruida* in 1803 and the drama *Le Désastre de Lisbonne* was produced, *mêlé de danse et de pantomime*, in Paris in 1804. Thereafter, its memory, outside Portugal, was kept alive in guide-books and travel-diaries, and only occasionally in nineteenth- and twentieth-century literature. There are many admirers of the works of Sir Arthur Quiller-Couch who remember the Lisbon earthquake through the vivid description of the disaster, based on the real adventures of Agnes Surriage and Sir Charles Henry Frankland,[33] in *Lady Good-For-Nothing* (1910), and there must also be many American and British readers of Oliver Wendell Holmes who have this two-hundred-year-old scrap of history fixed inescapably in their minds. Because on its hundredth anniversary:

> —there stood the stout old one-hoss-shay
> As fresh as on Lisbon-earthquake day.

For, as we have been told,

> It was on the terrible earthquake day
> That the Deacon finished the one-hoss-shay.

And then, a hundred years later, in 1855,

> First of November—the Earthquake-day
> There are traces of age in the one-hoss-shay,

and the end comes.

> First a shiver, and then a thrill,
> Then something decidedly like a spill,—
> And the parson was sitting upon a rock,
> At half-past nine by the meet'n'-house clock—
> Just the hour of the Earthquake shock!

[33] For this story, see Elias Nason: *Sir Charles Henry Frankland, Baronet: or Boston in Colonial Time.* Albany, N. Y., 1865, and Oliver Wendell Holmes, *Agnes.*

Bibliographical Note to Chapter Two

The numerous eyewitness accounts of the Lisbon earthquake are understandably confusing and contradictory,
particularly in the matter of the timing of the events of
the first day. I have not attempted to make a new study
of the earthquake and its effects, and this chapter is
mainly based on two works:

F. L. Pereira de Sousa: *O Terremoto do I° Novembro
de 1755 e um Estudo Demografico*. 4 vols. (especially vol. 3). Lisbon, 1919-32.

J. J. Moreira de Mendonça: *Historia Universal dos Terremotos . . . com uma narraçam individual do Terremoto do primeiro de Novembro de 1755 . . . em
Lisboa*. Lisbon, 1758.

This second work is the best of the contemporary accounts, and indeed it is a book of outstanding merit, in
my view excelling all previous studies of great earthquakes. I have, however, also made use of some other
contemporary material mentioned in Chapter Three, and
a number of recent topographical works published by the
Academia das Ciências de Lisboa and the Câmara Municipal of Lisbon:

Eduardo Freire de Oliveira: *Elementos para a história
do municipio de Lisboa*. Tomo XVI, pp. 133 ff. Lisbon, 1908.

Gustavo de Matos Sequeira: *Depois do Terremoto. Sub-*

sidios para a história dos bairros ocidentais de Lisboa. 4 vols. Lisbon, 1916-34.

Júlio de Castilho: *Lisboa Antiga: Bairros Orientais.* Second edition. 12 vols. Lisbon, 1934-38.

Gustavo de Matos Sequeira: *O Carmo e a Trindade.* 3 vols. Lisbon, 1939-41.

A. Vieira da Silva: *As Muralhas da Ribeira de Lisboa.* Second edition. 2 vols. Lisbon, 1940-41.

In addition, an important source of general, biographical, and topographical information is:

Esteves Pereira and Guilherme Rodrigues: *Portugal. Diccionario historico,* etc. 7 vols. Lisbon, 1904-15.

As regards bibliographies of the Lisbon earthquake, the most useful guide through the descriptive literature is the great work of Pereira de Sousa, mentioned above, which is packed with extracts from contemporary printed and manuscript accounts, and is fully annotated. Other Portuguese and foreign works will be found listed in the following publications:

Hans Woerle: *Der Erschütterungsbezirk des grossen Erdbebens zu Lissabon.* Münchener geographische Studien, ed. S. Günther, VIII (1900), pp. 6 ff., pp. 22 ff.

F. de Montessus de Ballore: *Bibliografia general de temblores y terremotos.* Vol. I, 1570 ff.; Vol. VII, 6738 ff., 8662 ff. Santiago de Chile, 1915-19.

Catálogo, second edition, of the Exposição Comemorativa do Terremoto de 1755. Lisbon, 1934.

Charles Davison: *Great Earthquakes,* pp. 27-28. London, 1936.

For modern scientific accounts of the Lisbon earthquake in English see:

Harry Fielding Reid: *The Lisbon Earthquake of November 1, 1755. Bull. Seismological Society of America*, IV, No. 2 (June 1914), p. 53.

Charles Davison: *op. cit.*, p. 27. Excellent for the English eyewitness accounts and contemporary scientific discussion.

Three of the English narratives stand out above others as vivid and informative accounts of the disaster:

Mr. Braddock: For his adventures, see John Athelstane Smith, Conde da Carnota. *Marquis of Pombal*, p. 51. Second edition, 1871; also printed by Charles Davy. *Letters . . . upon Subjects of Literature*, II p. 12 (1787).

Thomas Chase: *Gentleman's Magazine*, LXXXIII (1813), pp. 105-10, 201-06, 314-17. The earthquake took place on the twenty-sixth birthday of this young man, who was very badly injured.

Mr. Fowke: *A genuine Letter to Mr. Joseph Fowke from his brother near Lisbon*. London, 1755? This vigorous and most interesting letter is dated 17 November 1755. Mr. Fowke (or ?Fowkes) lived in the Cidade Baixa near the Church of São Nicolau.

To Dr. Davison's bibliography, keeping principally to the English material, I would add:

Baretti, J.: *Journey from London to Genoa*, I, pp. 137 ff. Third edition, 1770.

Boxer, Professor C. R.: *Pombal's Dictatorship and the Great Lisbon Earthquake, 1755. History Today*, V, No. 11 (November 1955).

Cheke, Marcus: *Dictator of Portugal*, pp. 62 ff. London, 1938. This is the best general account of the disaster in English, and the preceding chapters should also be read as historical background to the earthquake.

Estorninho, Carlos: *O Terremoto de 1755 e a sua repercussão nas relaçoes Luso-Britanicas.* Lisbon, 1956.

Keene, Sir Benjamin: *Private Correspondence.* Ed. Richard Lodge. London, 1933.

Macaulay, Rose: *They Went to Portugal,* pp. 267 ff.; also pp. 203 ff. London, 1946.

Walford, A. R.: *The British Community in Lisbon c. 1755.* Hist. Assoc. Lisbon Branch. 10th Annual Report (1946-50), p. 639.

Periodicals: In addition to the *Philosophical Transactions of the Royal Society* and the *Gentleman's Magazine,* cited by Davison, note also: *London Evening Post,* No. 4375 (22-25 November) ff.; *London Gazette,* No. 9532 (25-29 November) ff.; *London Magazine,* vols. xxiv, xxv, *passim.; Public Advertiser,* No. 6576 (25 November) ff.; *Scots Magazine,* vols. xvii, xviii, *passim.; Whitehall Evening Post,* No. 1521 (22-29 November) ff.

Addendum to Bibliographies

Catálogo, Exposição iconográfica e bibliográfica comemorativa da reconstrução da cidade depois do terremoto de 1755.
Palácio Galveias. Lisbon, 1955.
Publn. of the Câmara Municipal de Lisboa.

INDEX